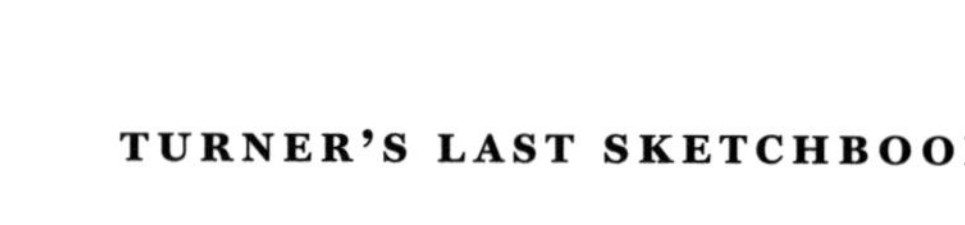

TURNER'S LAST SKETCHBOOK

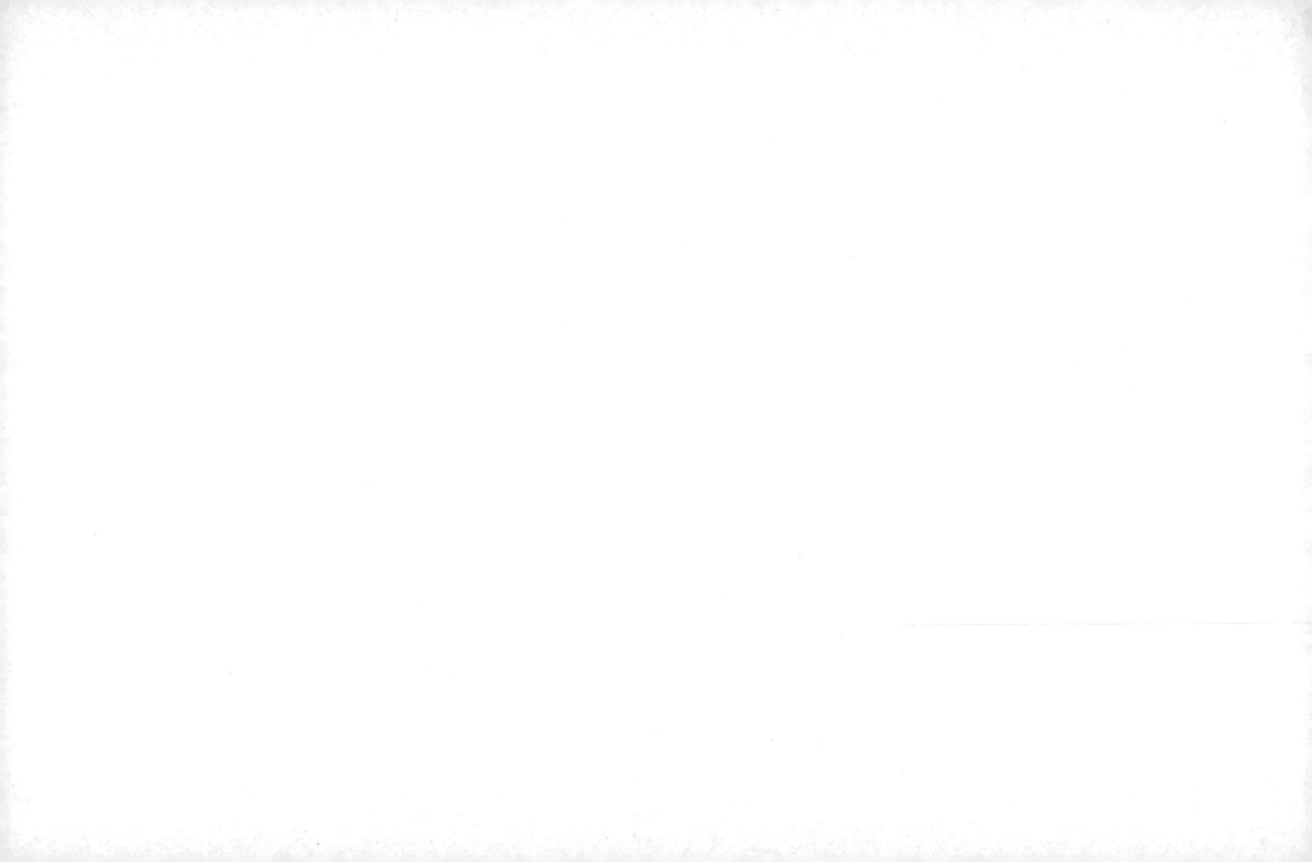

Turner's Last Sketchbook

WITH A POEM BY TRACEY EMIN

YALE CENTER FOR BRITISH ART

From the Director

YALE CENTER FOR BRITISH ART is deeply grateful to all who contributed to this publication.

We are indebted to Tracey Emin for her love poem, which bridges Turner's world and ours. Emin's poem, written for this volume, belongs to a distinct body of text-based works of art—painted, drawn, printed in ink, or transformed into neon signs—whose raw materials derive from her personal life. This one responds to Turner's sketchbook and reiterates their shared connection to Margate, where Emin was raised and where she has recently returned to champion the city as a destination for artists. This spiritually aligns her with Turner, who knew the seaside town from his youth and drew inspiration from its coastline throughout his life.

Turner and Emin are also connected by their fellowship in the Royal Academy of Arts. Turner was the academy's Professor of Perspective from 1807 to 1837 and served as its acting president in the summer of 1845—the very time he was using the sketchbook reproduced here. Emin was elected to the academy in 2007 and served as Eranda Professor of Drawing from 2011 to 2013. She has the distinction of being one of the first female professors appointed since the Royal Academy's founding in 1768.

We are grateful to Martina Droth, Deputy Director and Chief Curator, for liaising with Tracey Emin and her studio. Additionally, we appreciate the departments of Advancement, Design, Imaging Services, Prints and Drawings, and Publications at the Yale Center for British Art; the printer, Trifolio; and our distributor, Yale University Press, for bringing this volume to fruition. Through this facsimile, Turner's sketchbook can now inspire on a scale that the artist likely would never have conceived.

Courtney J. Martin
Paul Mellon Director
Yale Center for British Art

J. M. W. Turner used this sketchbook from June to September 1845. It consists of eighty-eight leaves with sketches in watercolor and graphite on medium, slightly textured, machine-made wove paper, bound in red leather with a brass clasp.

All leaves left blank by Turner have been reproduced in this volume.

The endpaper with the stationer's label indicates the front of the sketchbook, suggesting that Turner filled the first three-quarters of the right-hand leaves with watercolors before rotating the book to make additional sketches.

Another possibility is that Turner started from the other end of the book with notes and sketches in pencil. At some point after Turner's death, twenty-one leaves in this portion of the book (68 v – 88 v) were hand-numbered based on this interpretation.

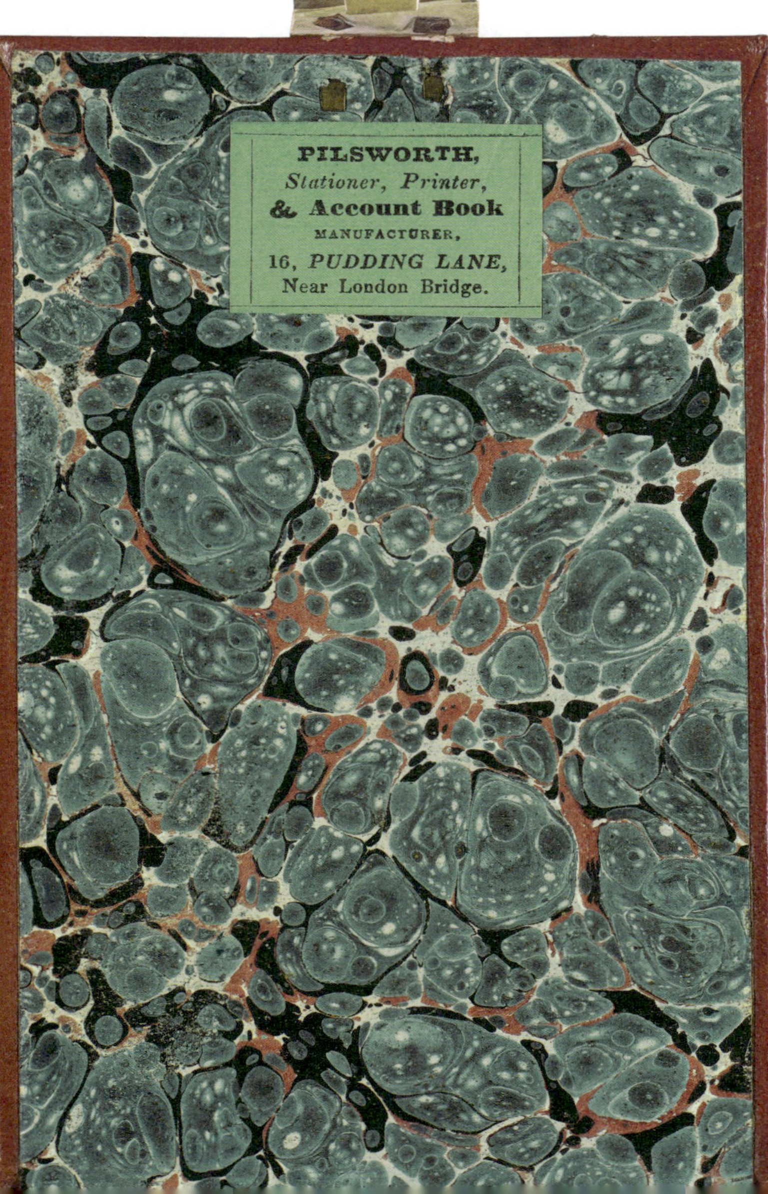
PILSWORTH,
Stationer, Printer,
& Account Book
MANUFACTURER,
16, PUDDING LANE,
Near London Bridge.

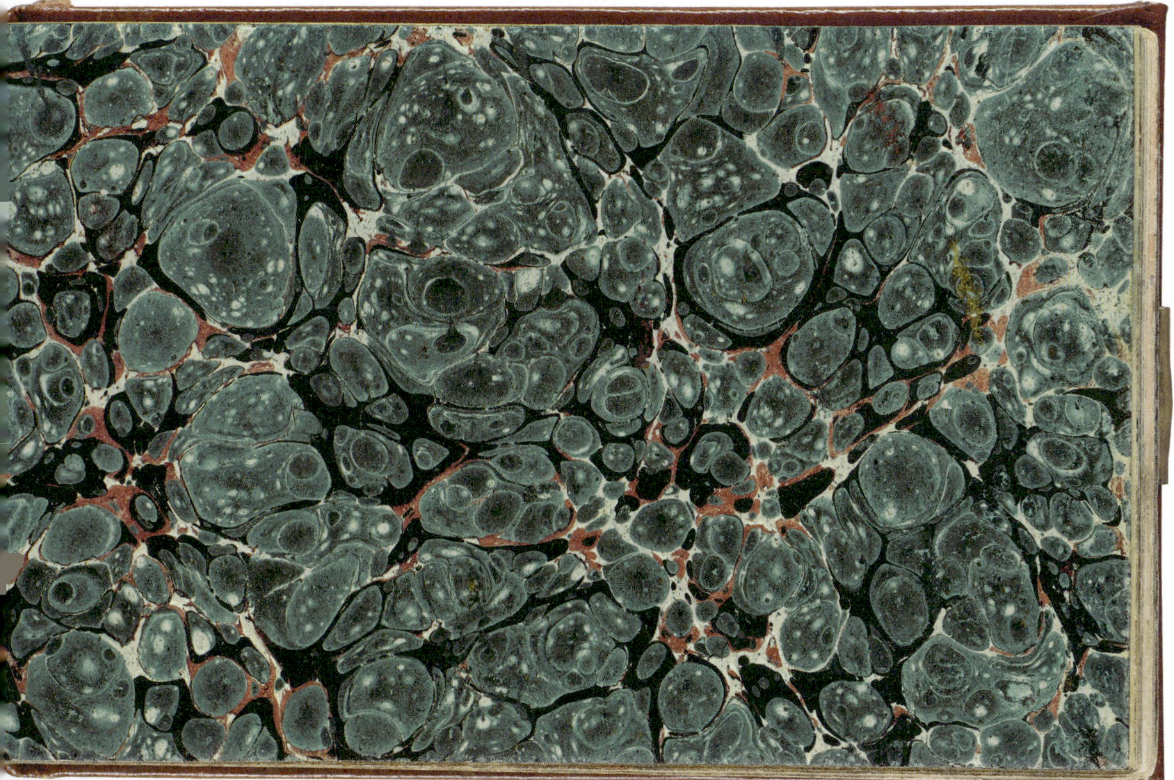

Sketch Book of Turner's –

1R

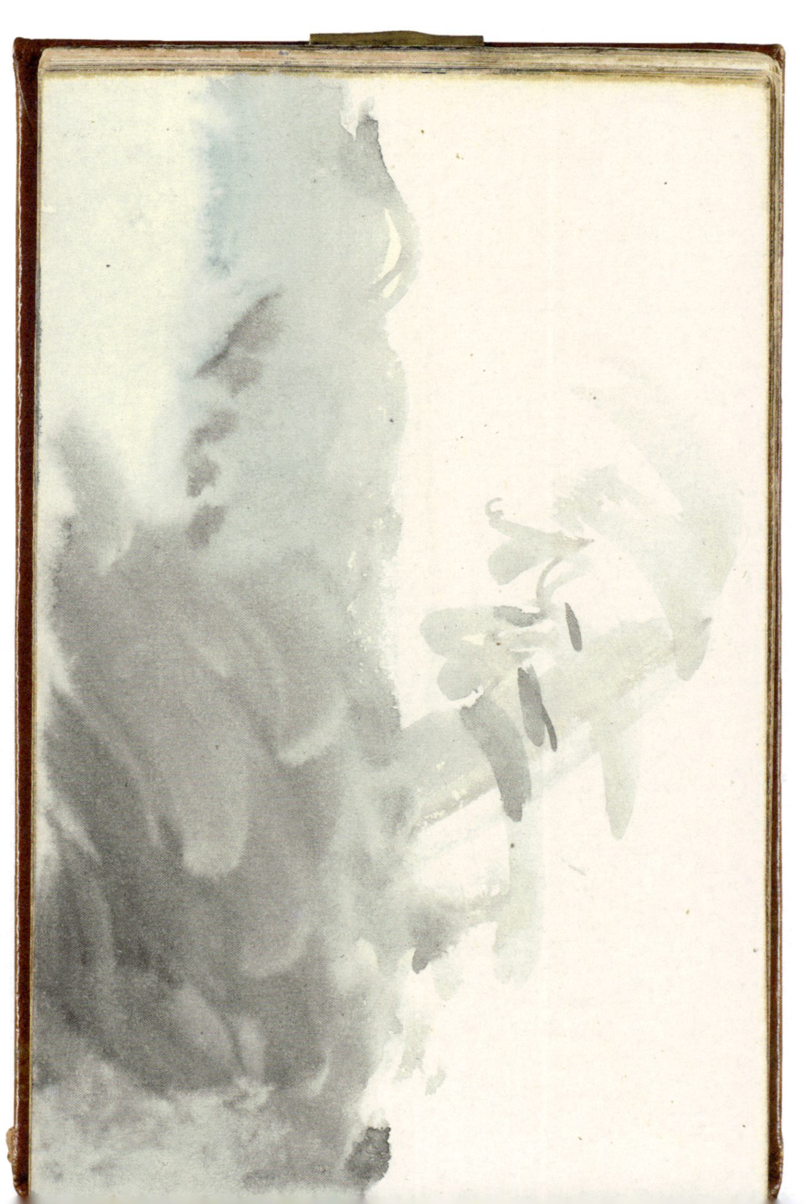

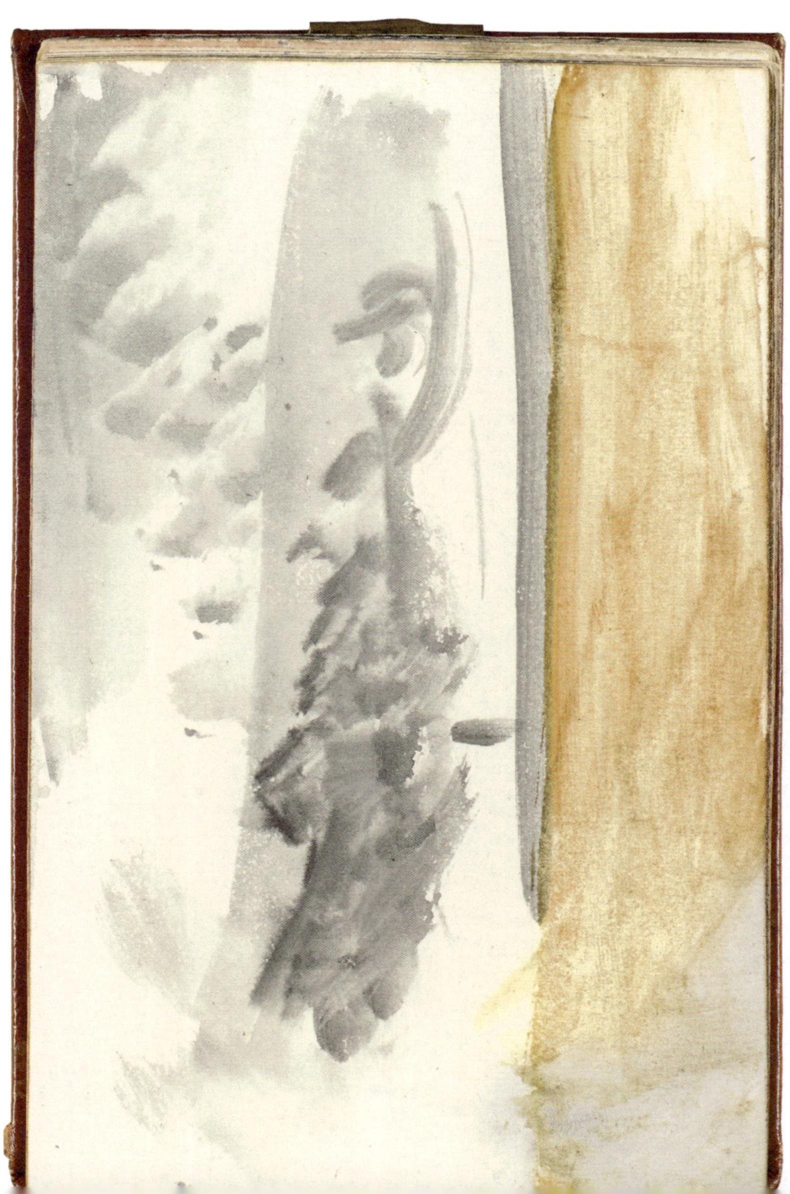

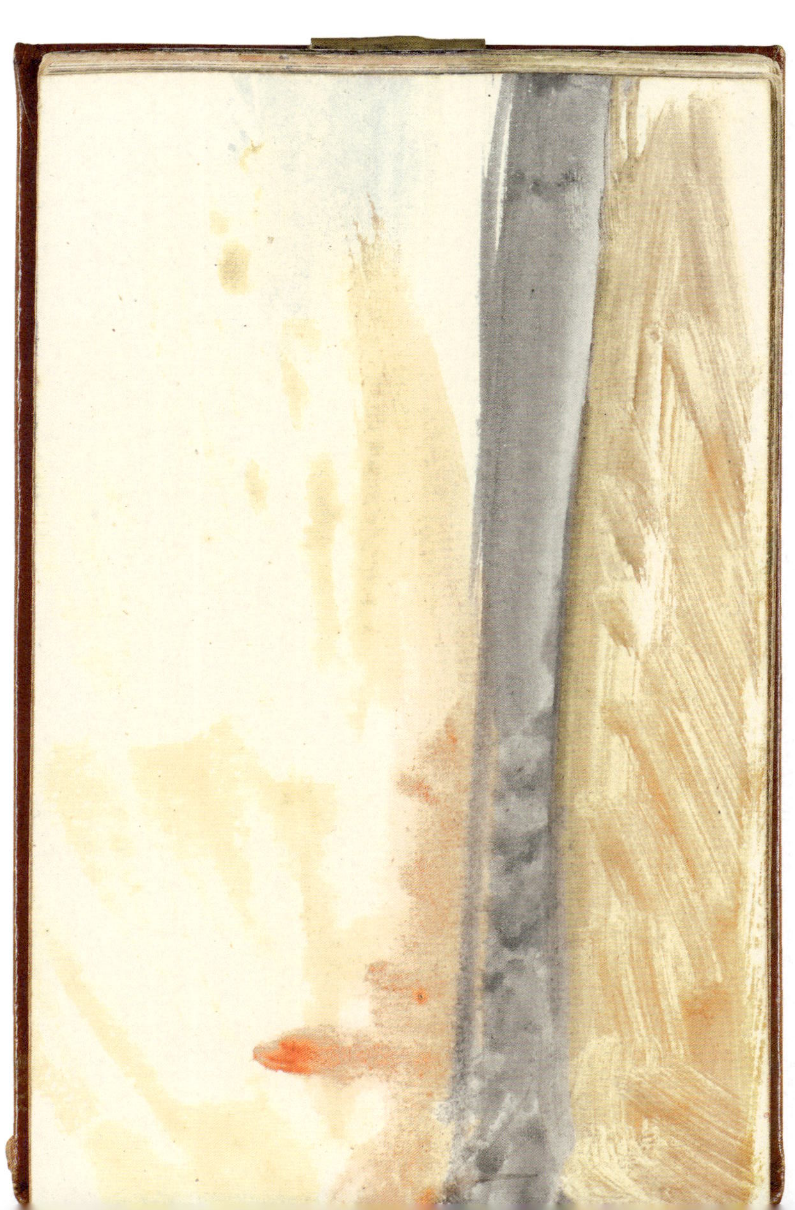

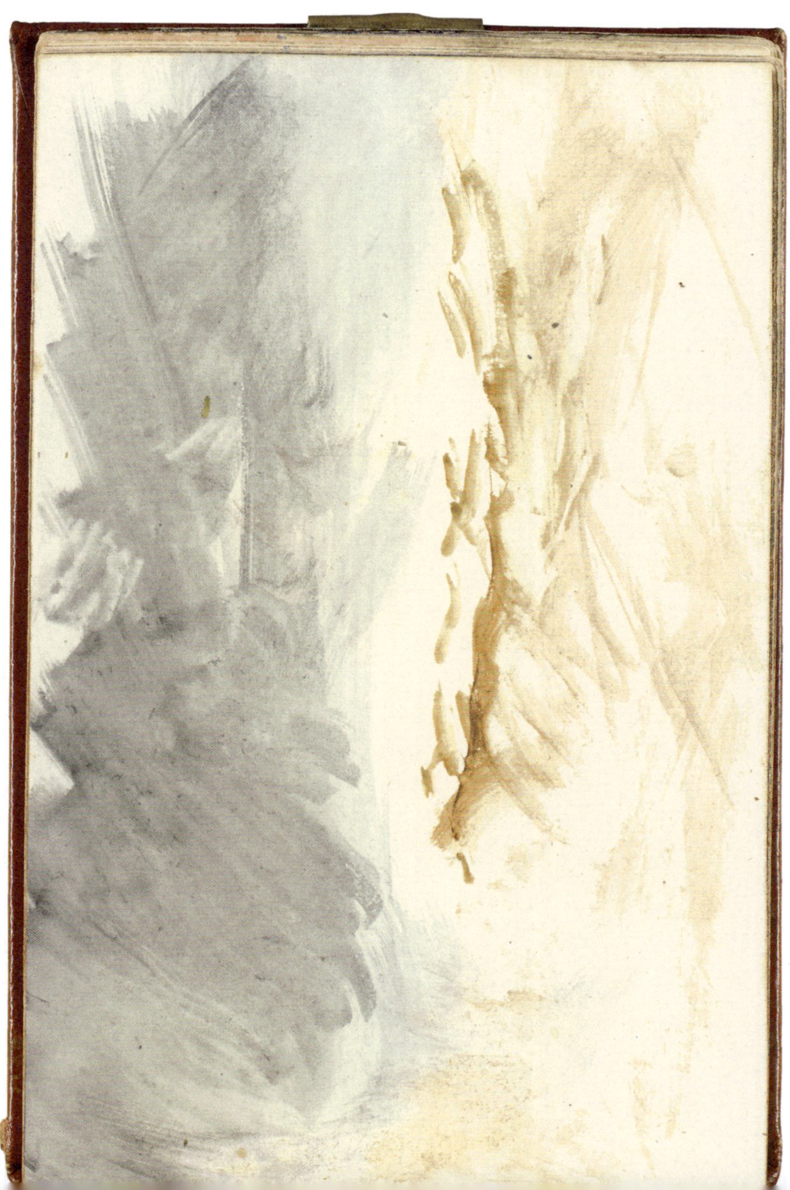

4v

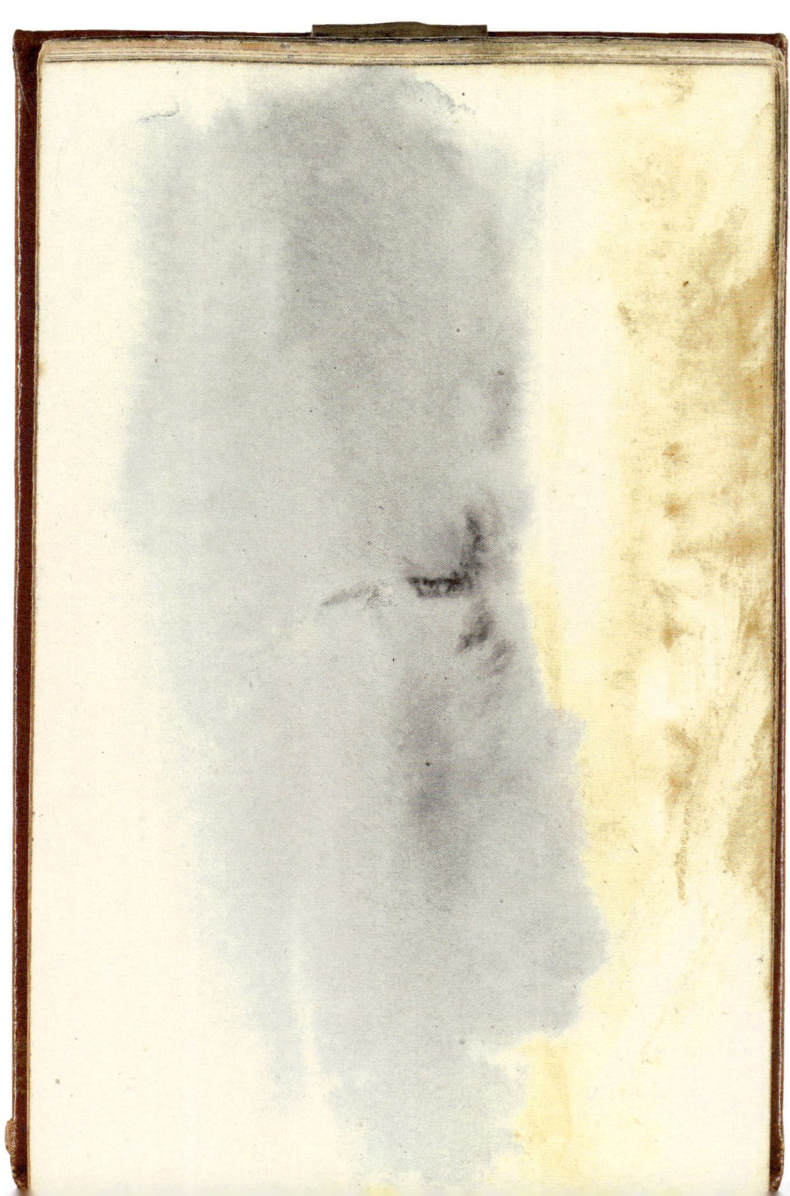

5v

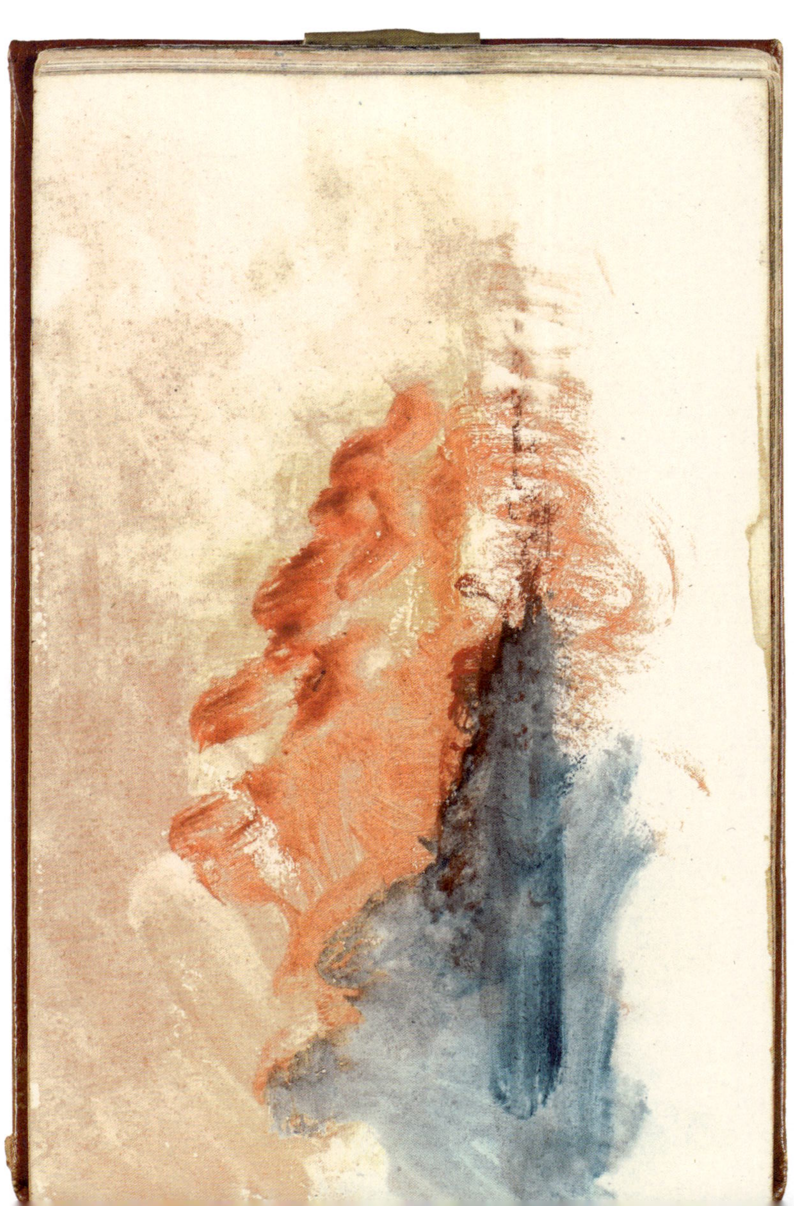

7R

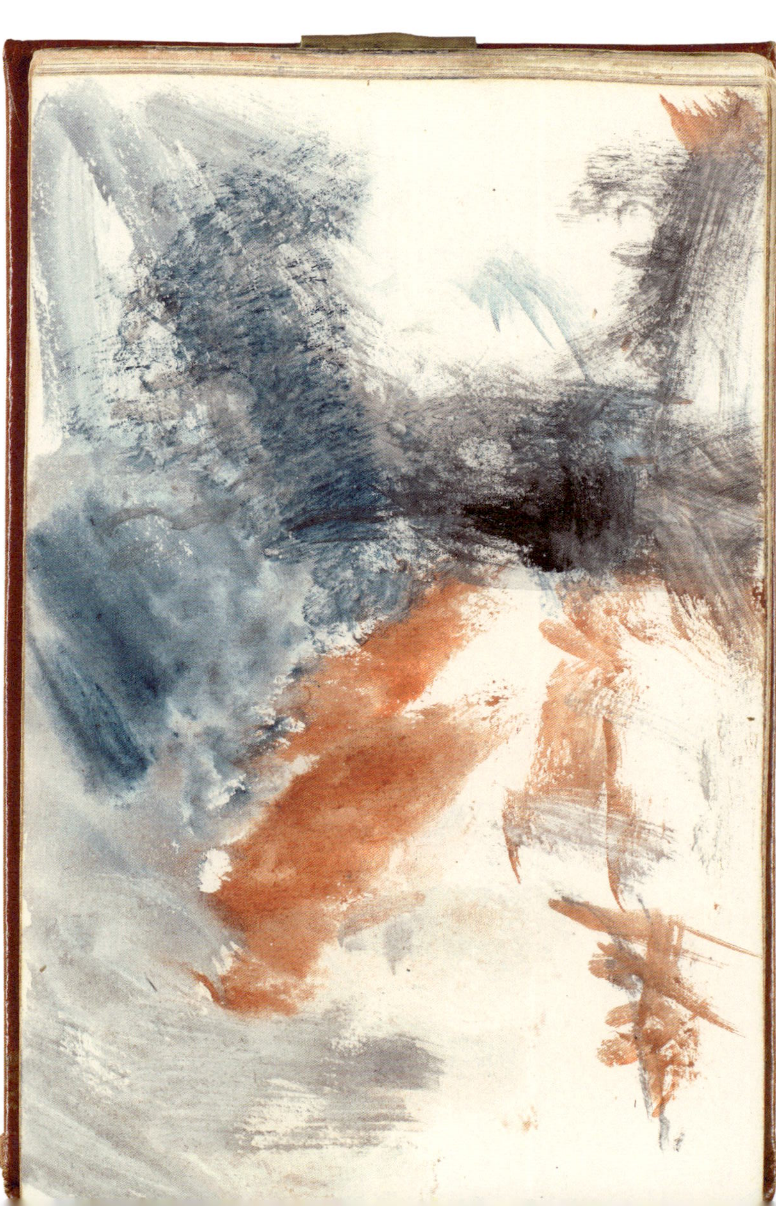

8R

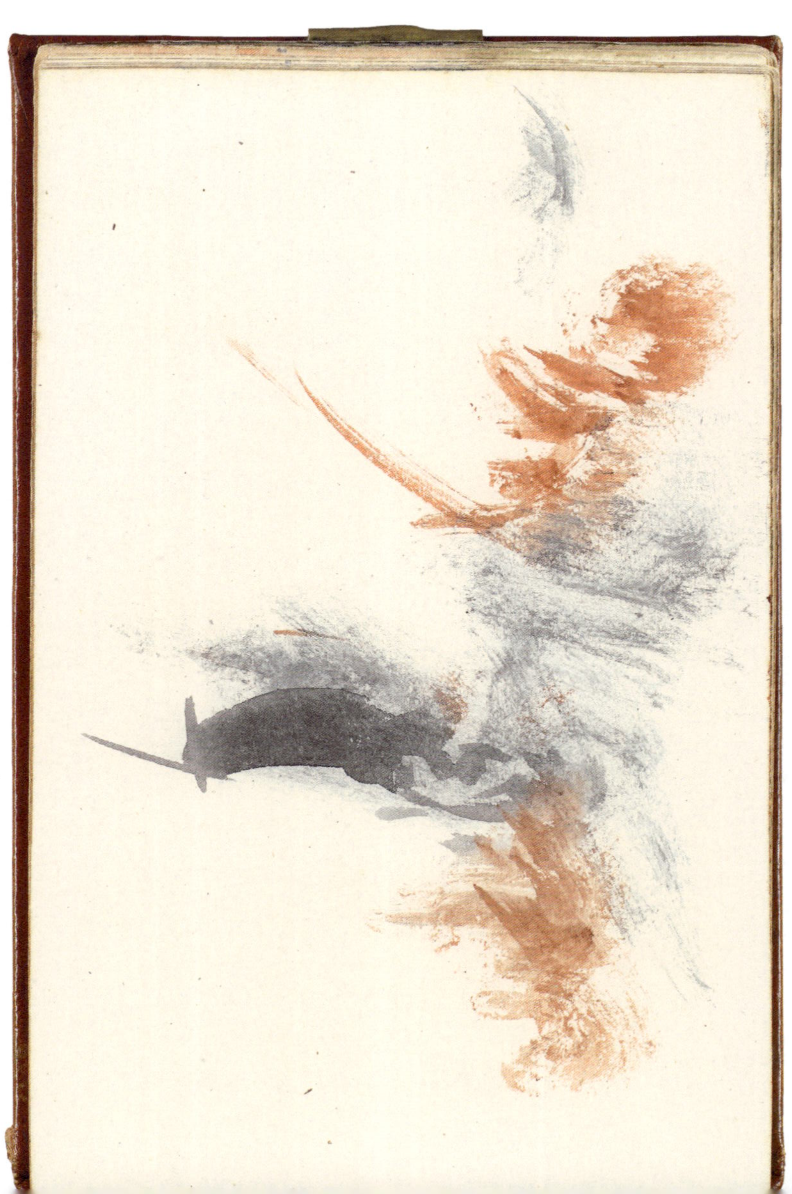

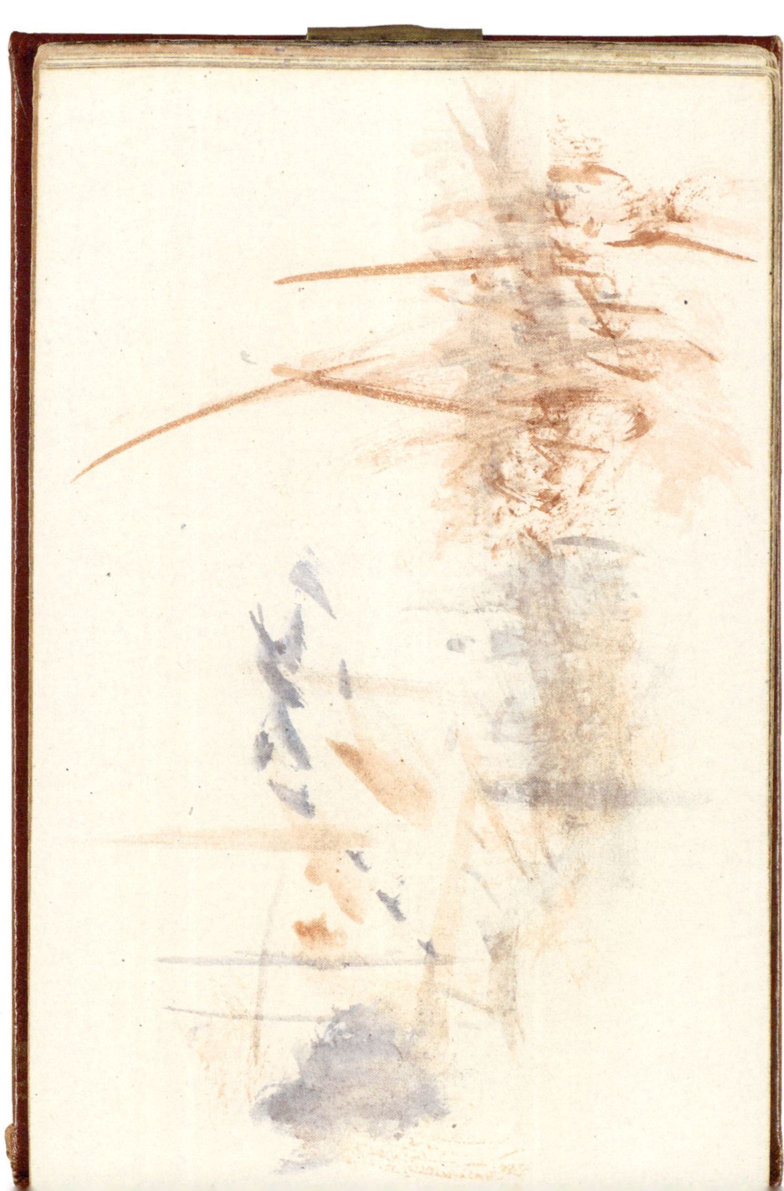

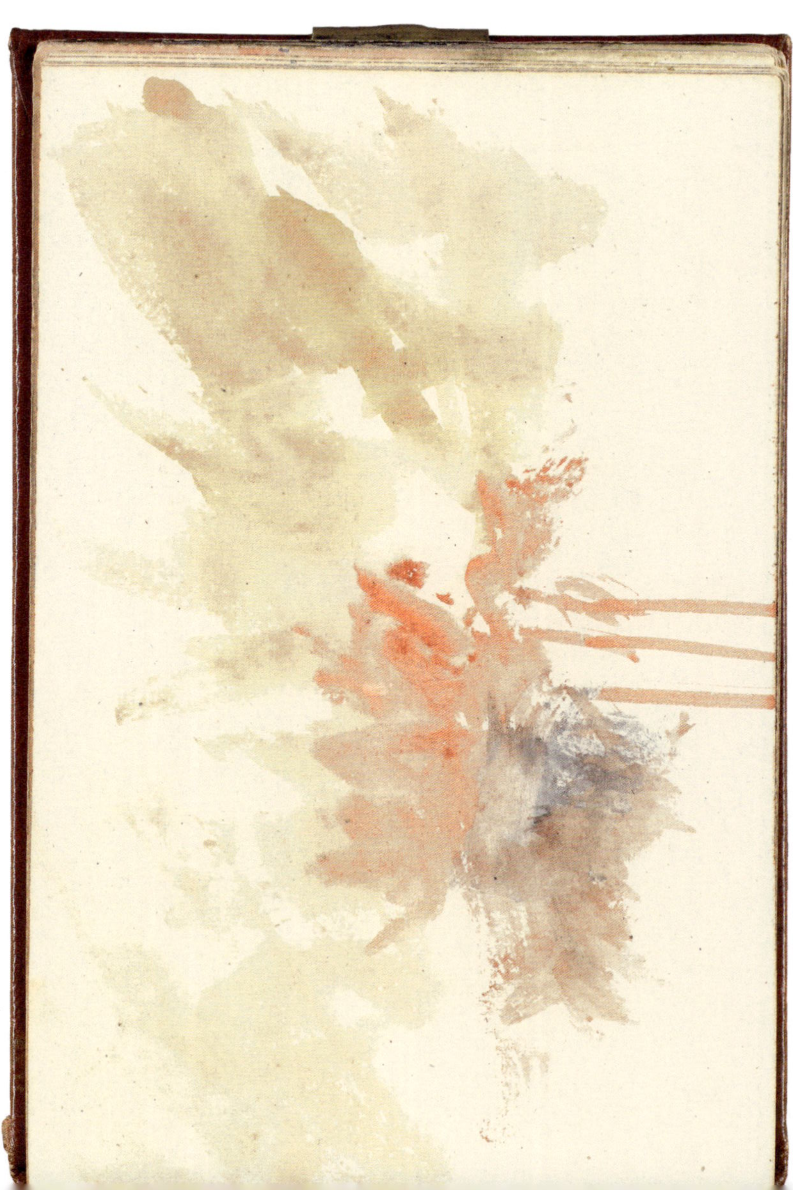

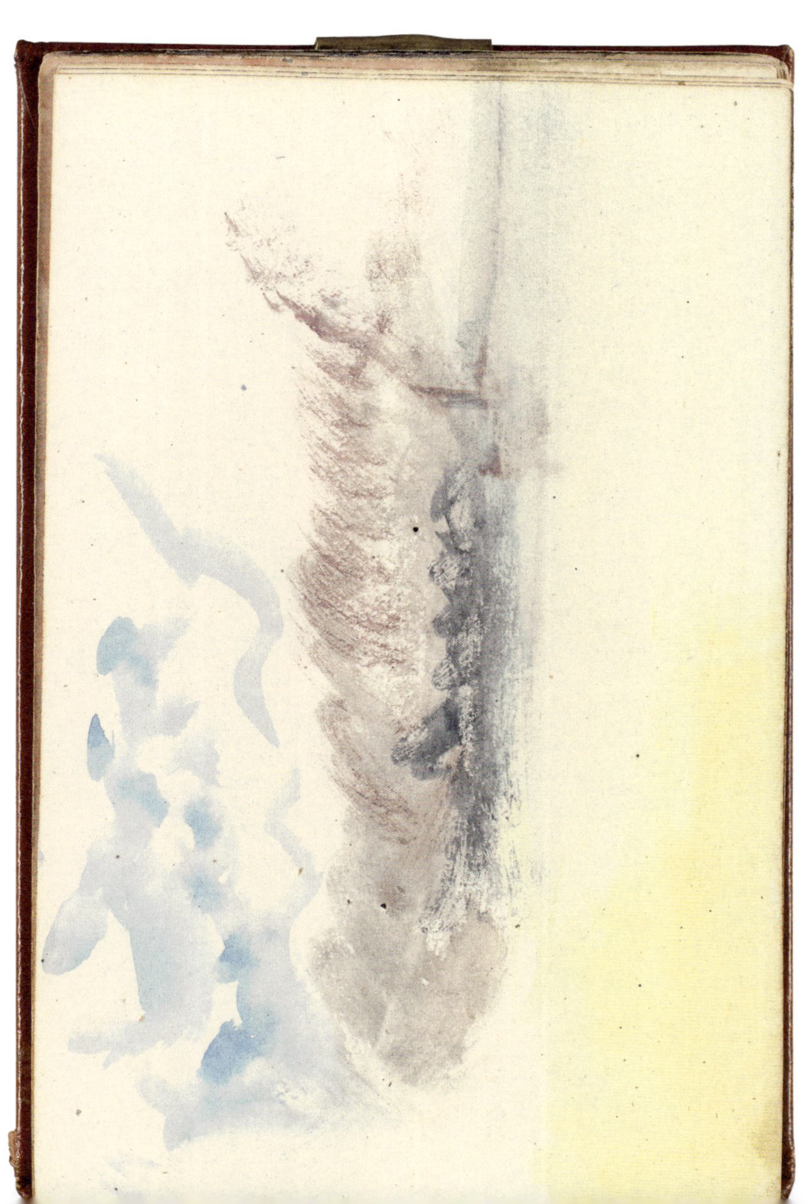

13 R

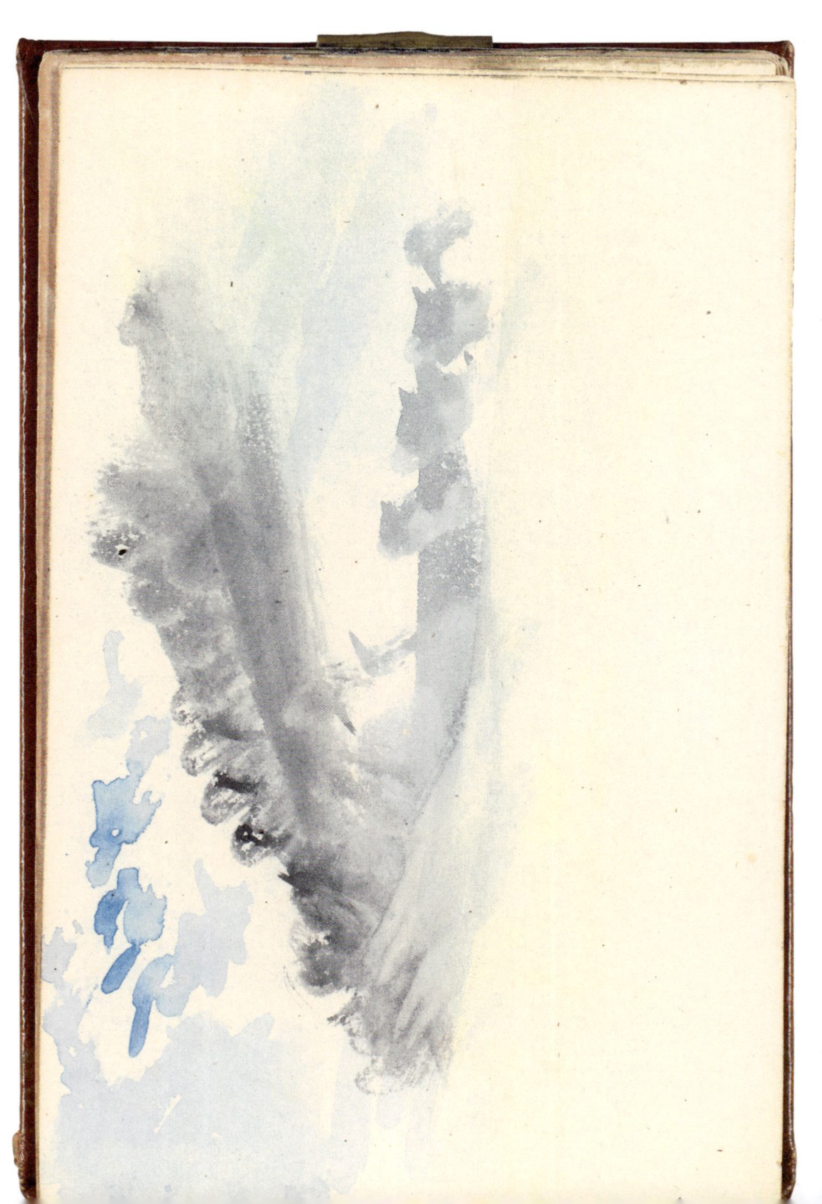

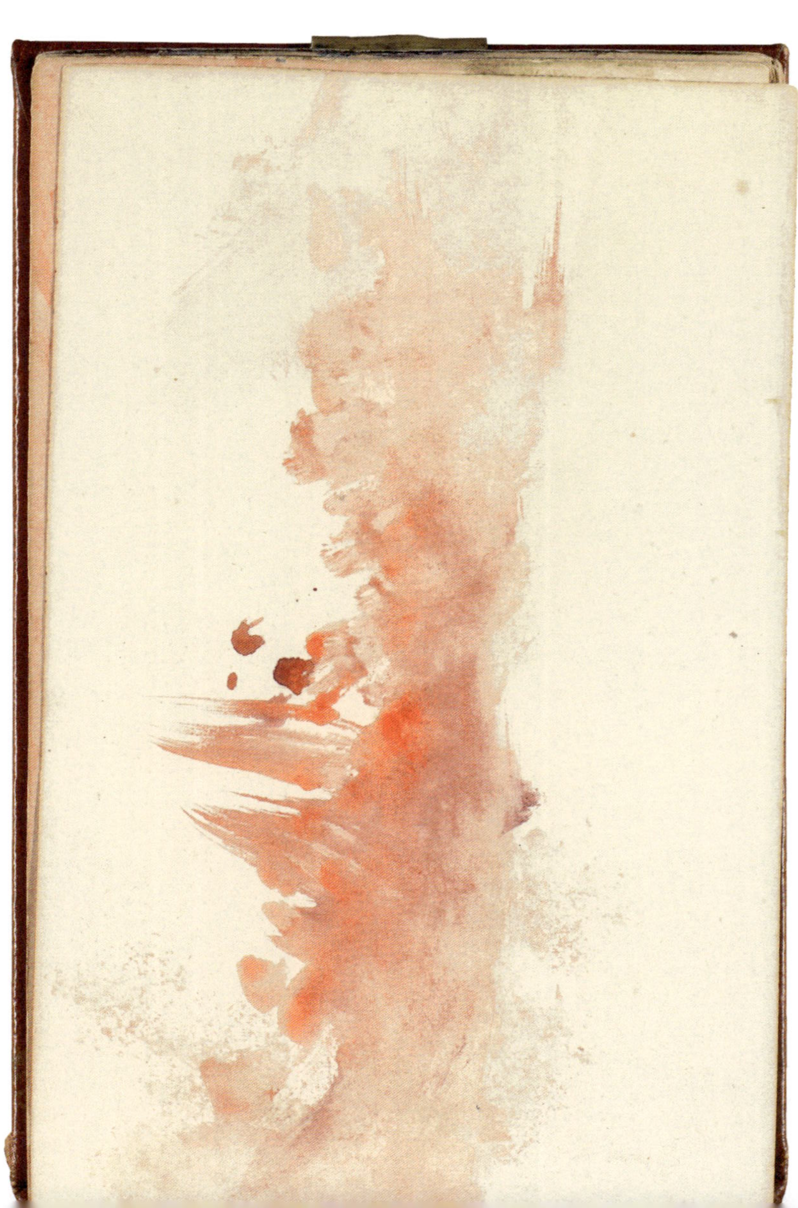

14v

15 R

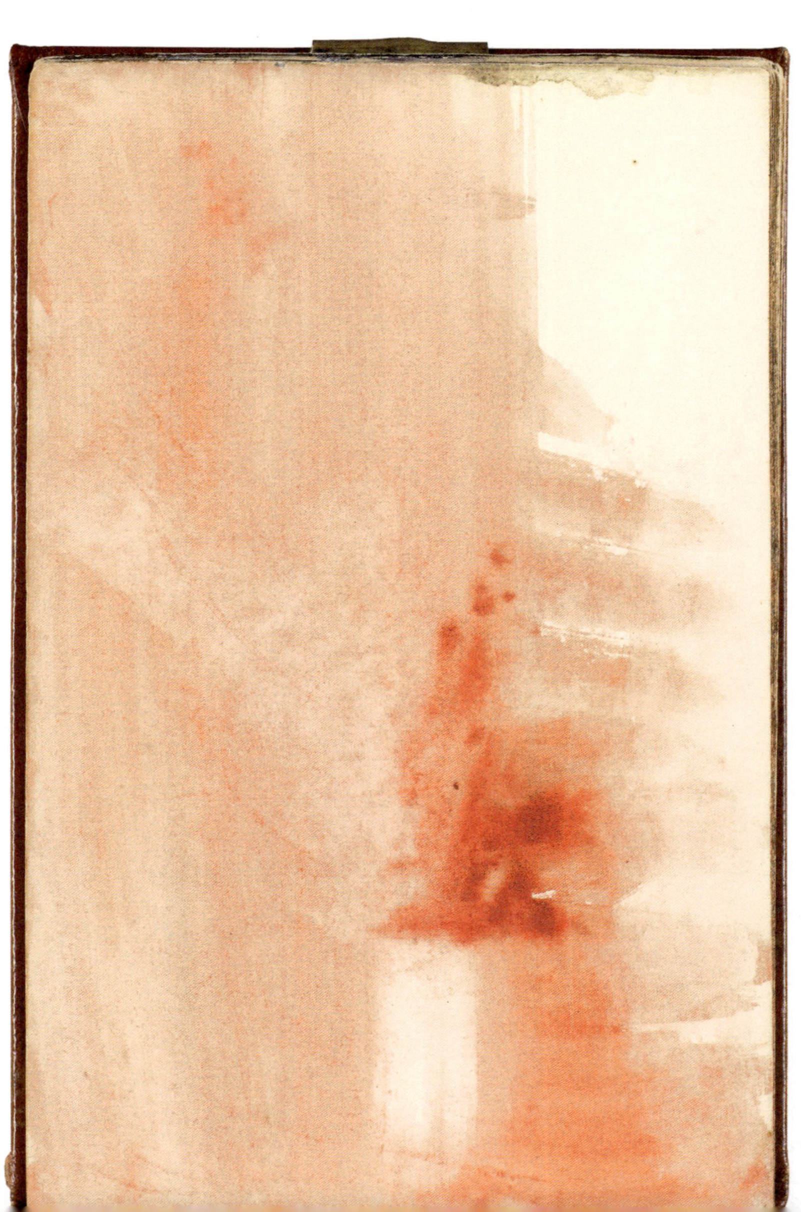

16 R

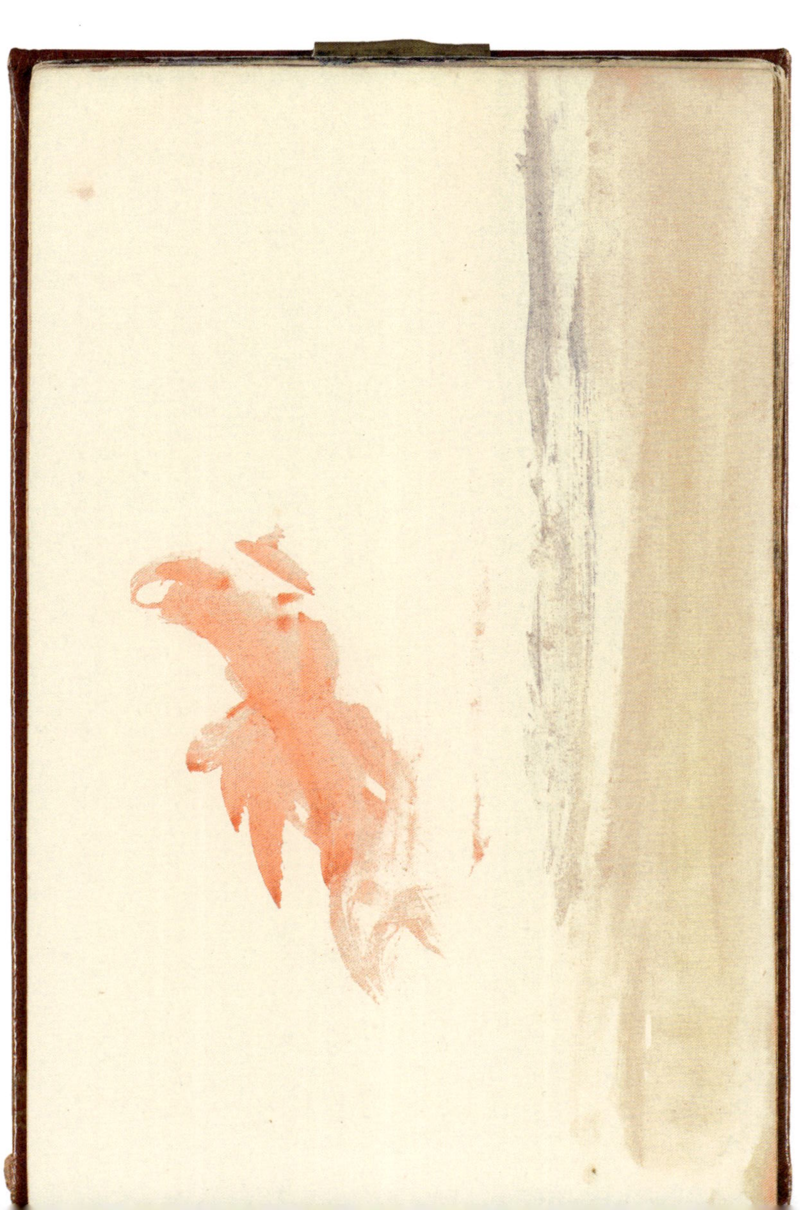

16 v

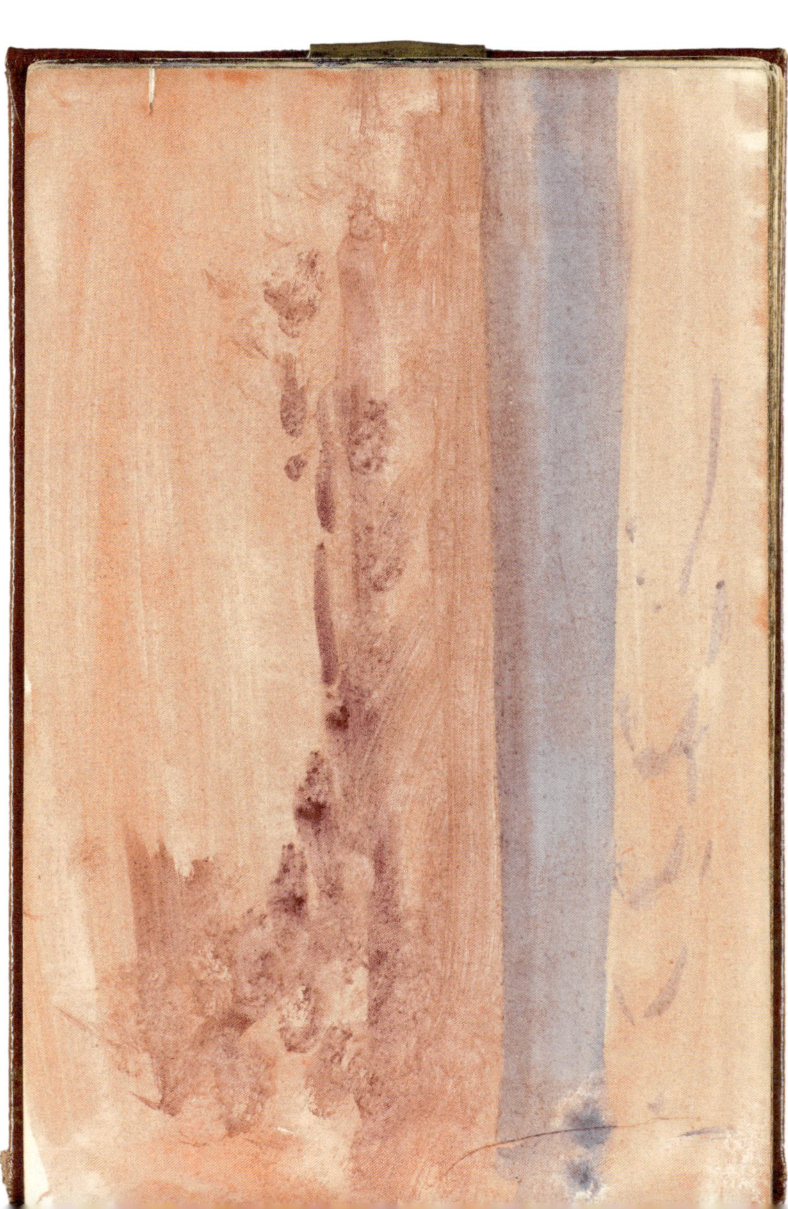

18 R

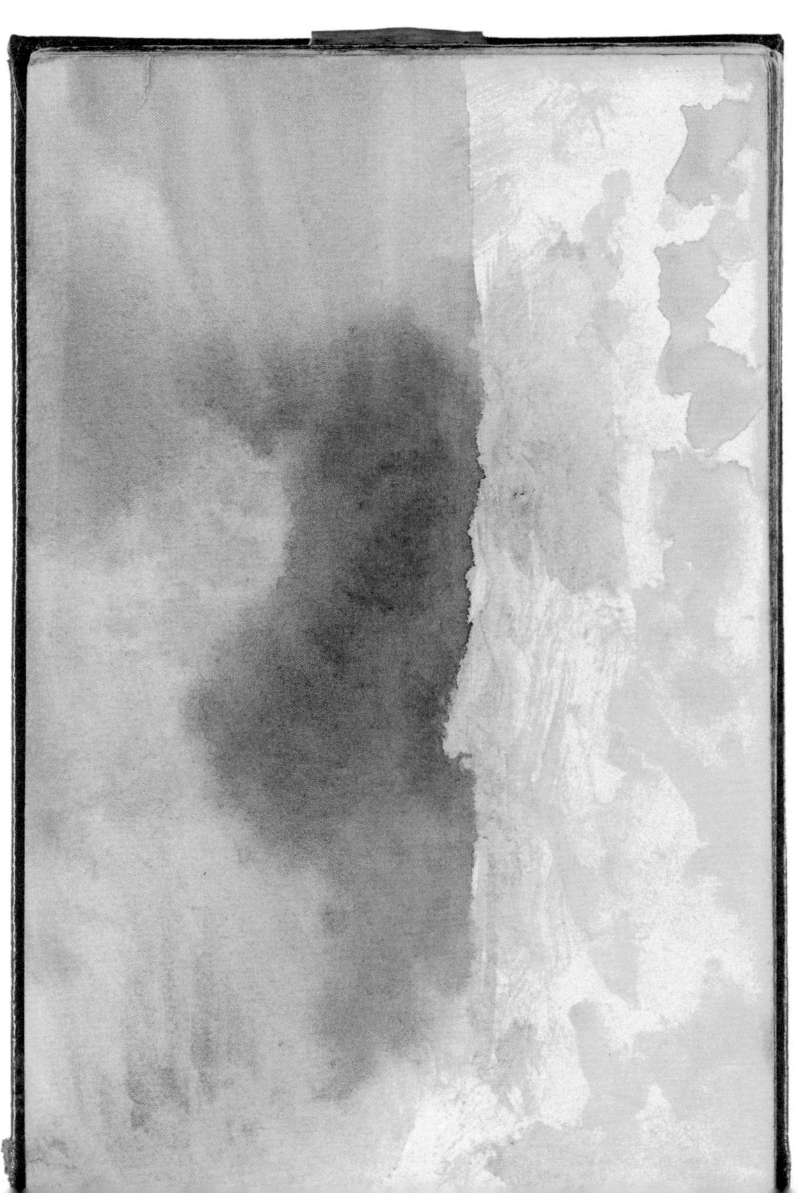

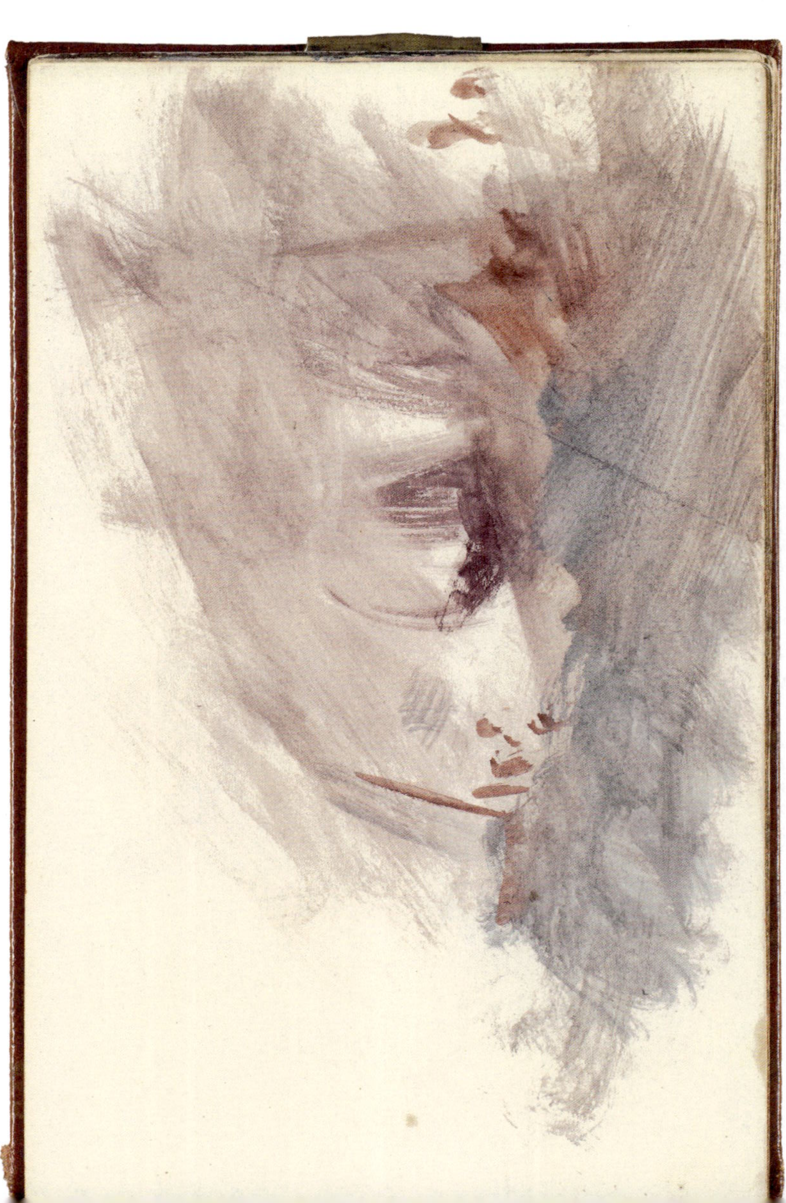

21 R

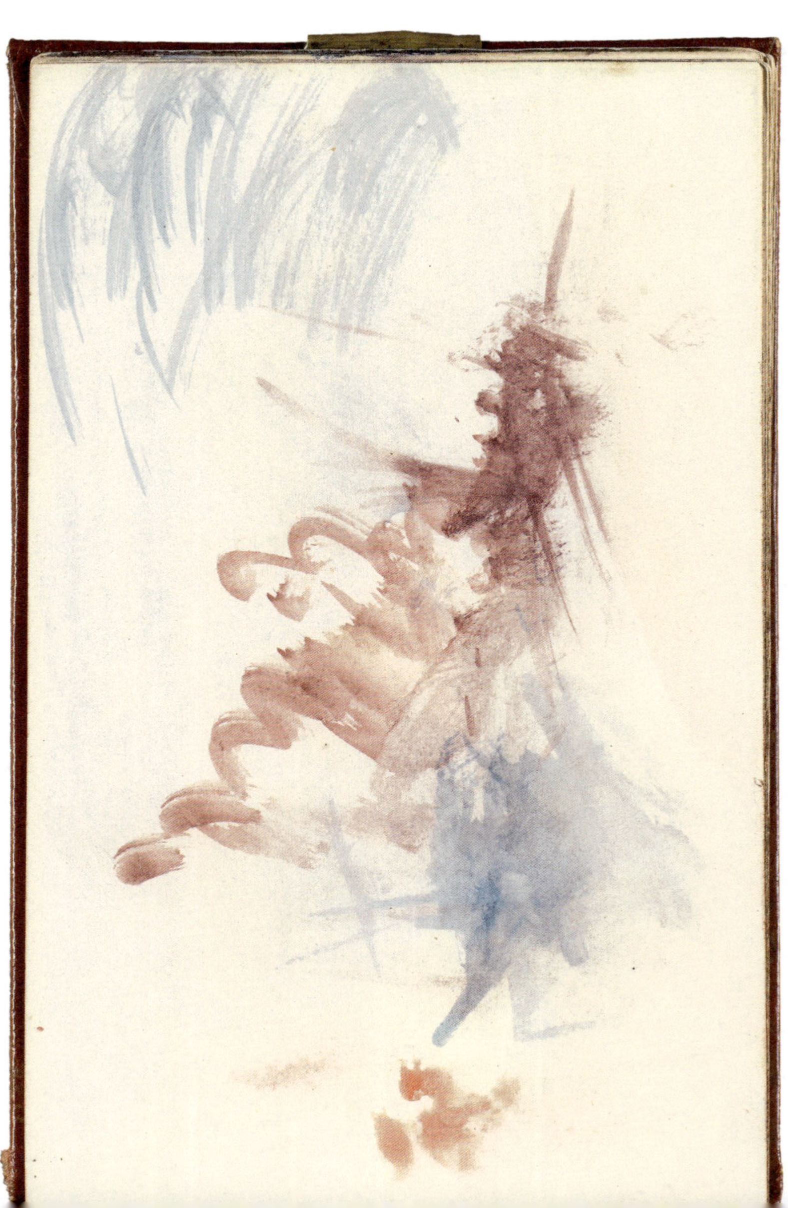

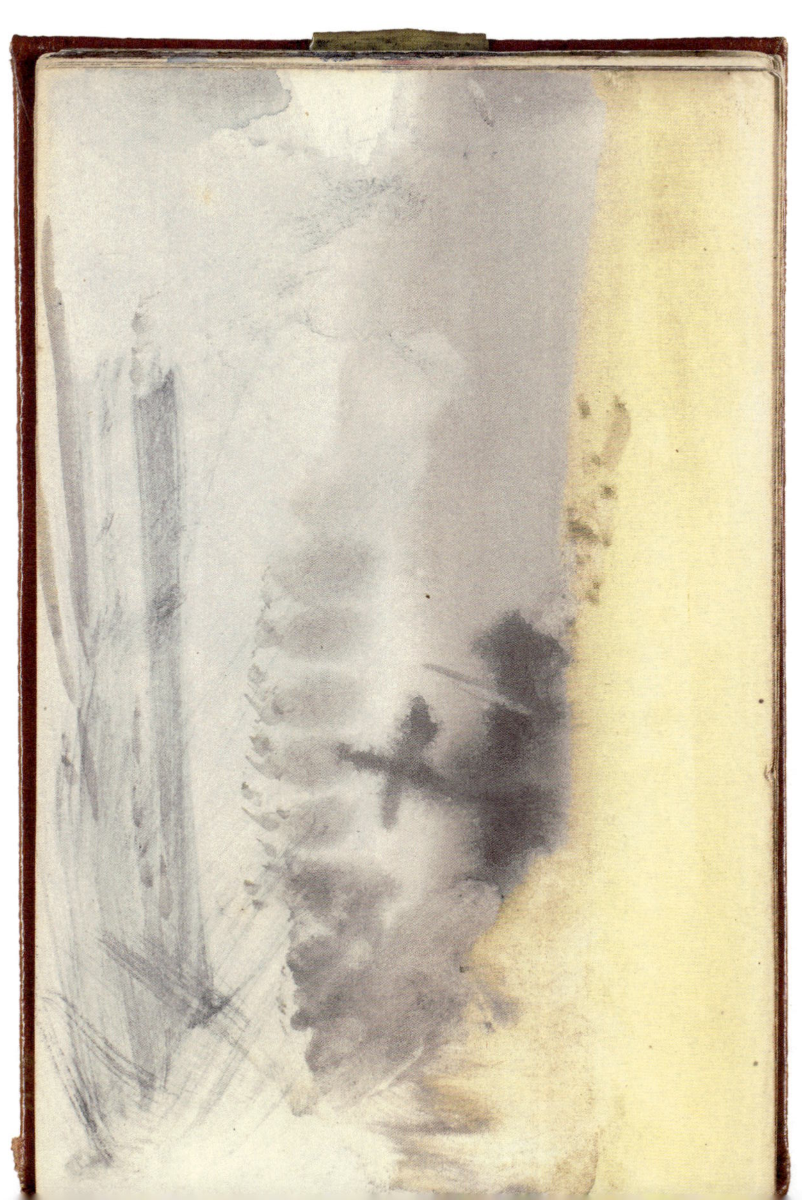

22 V

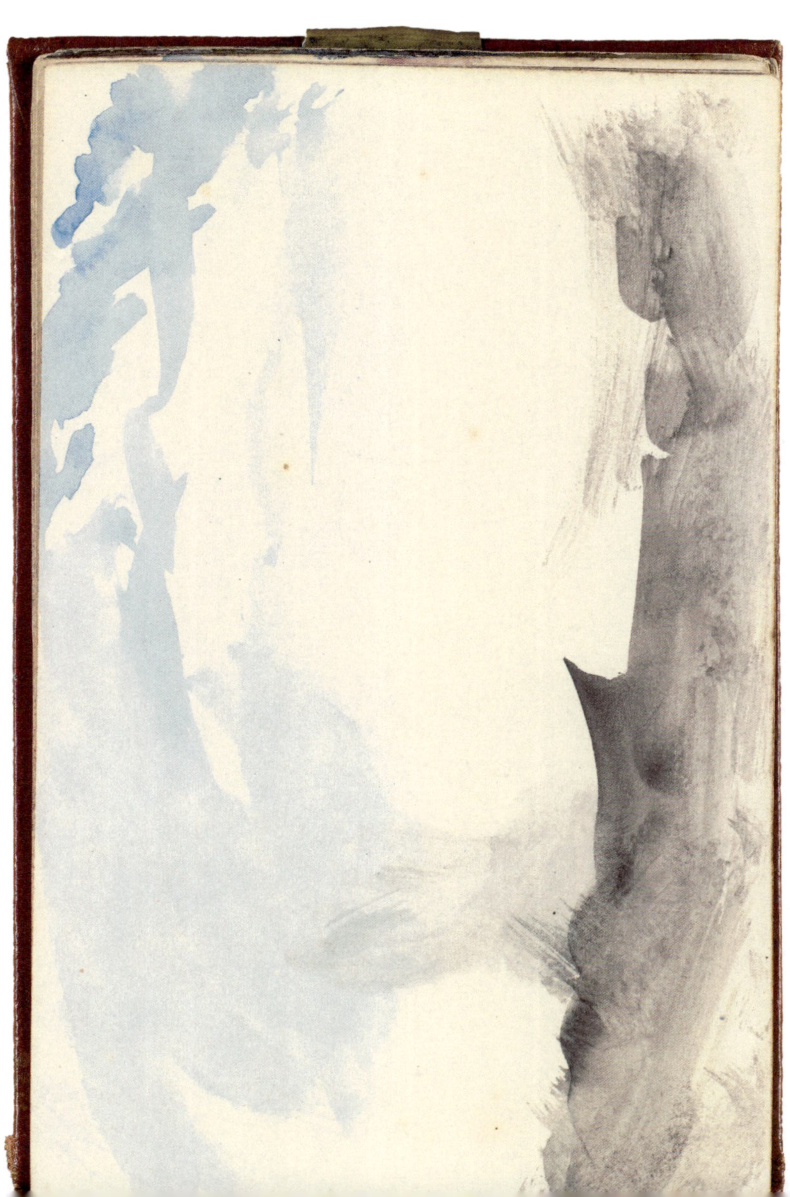

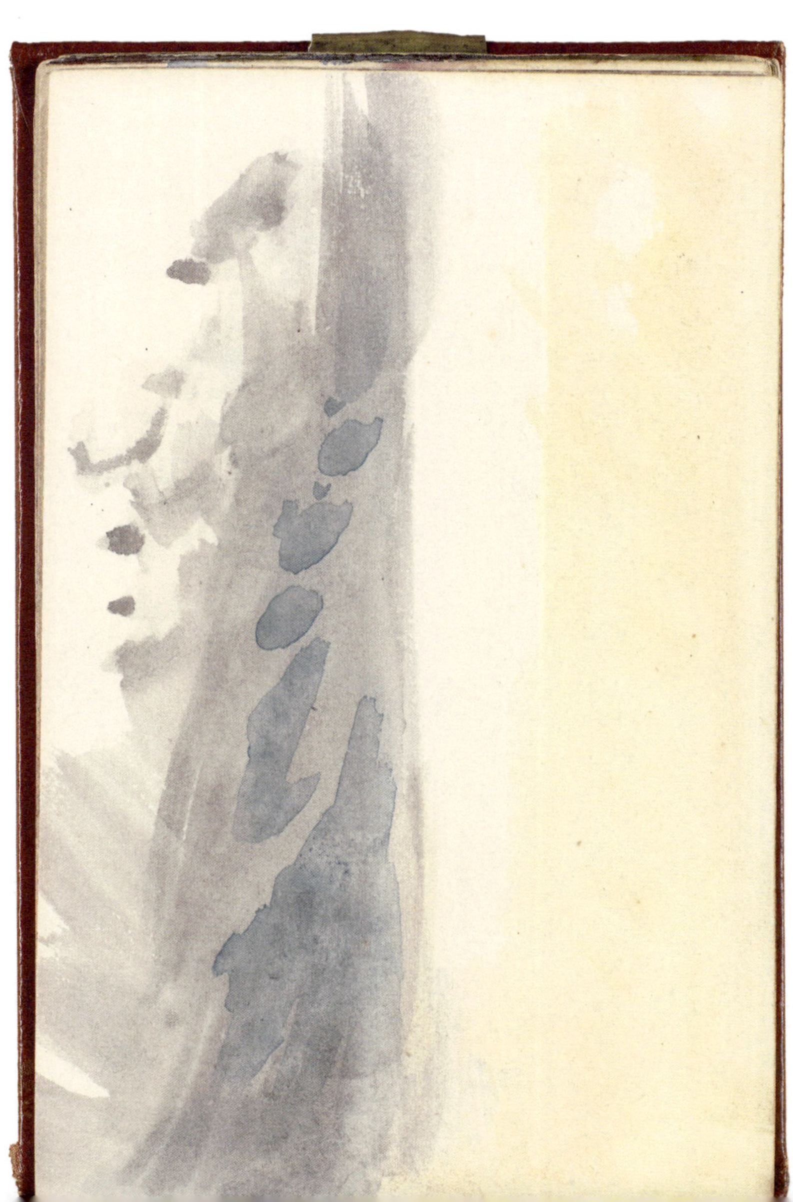

28 R

29 R

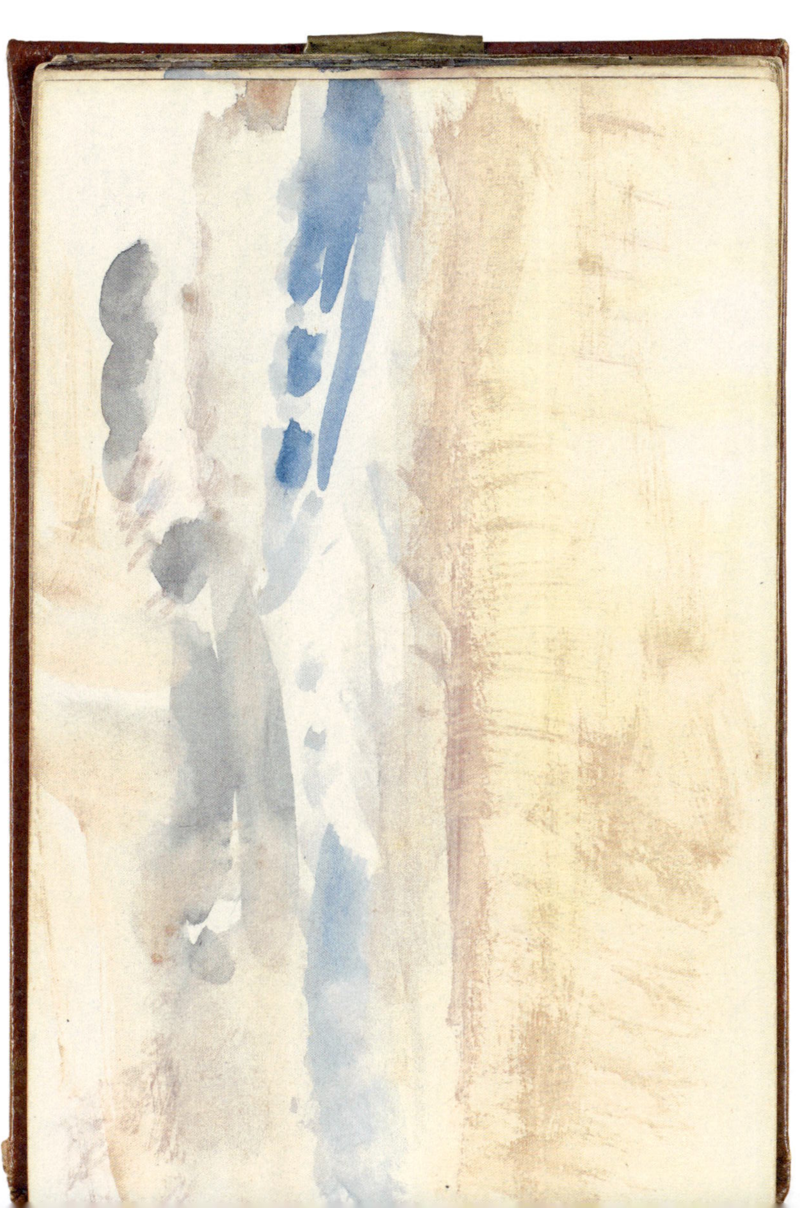

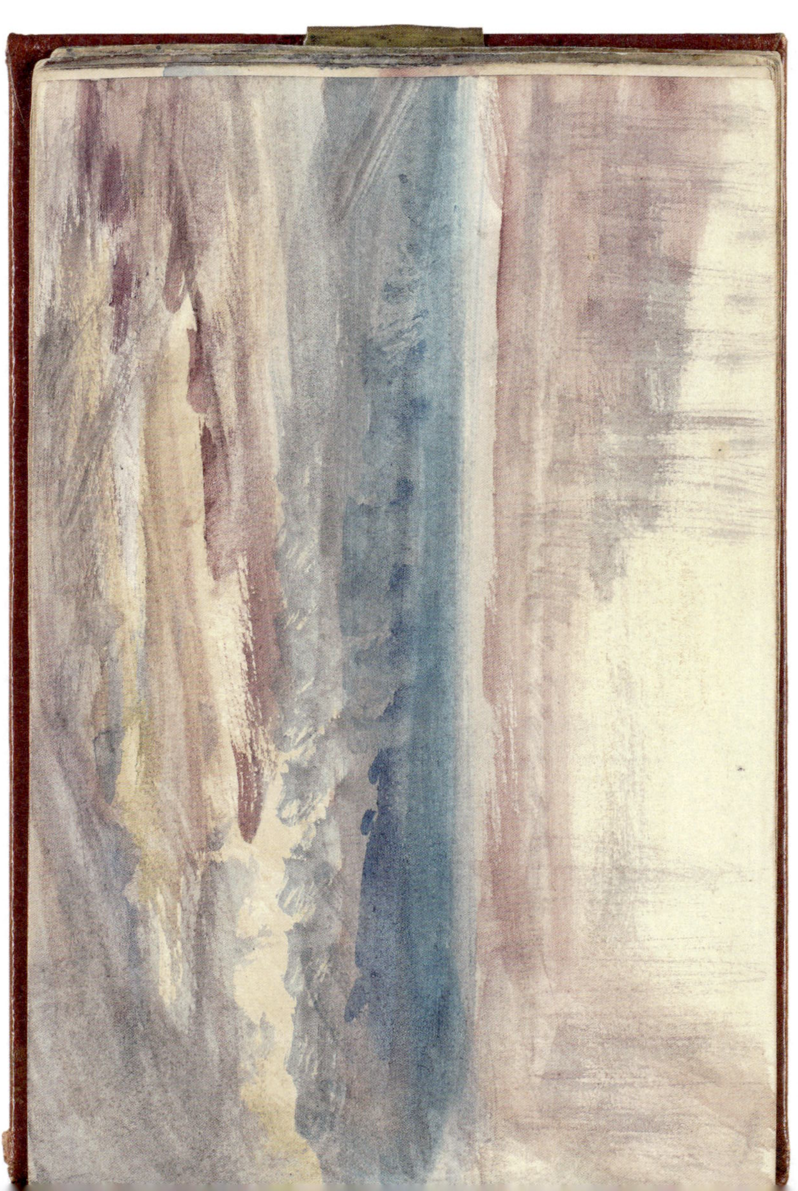

31R

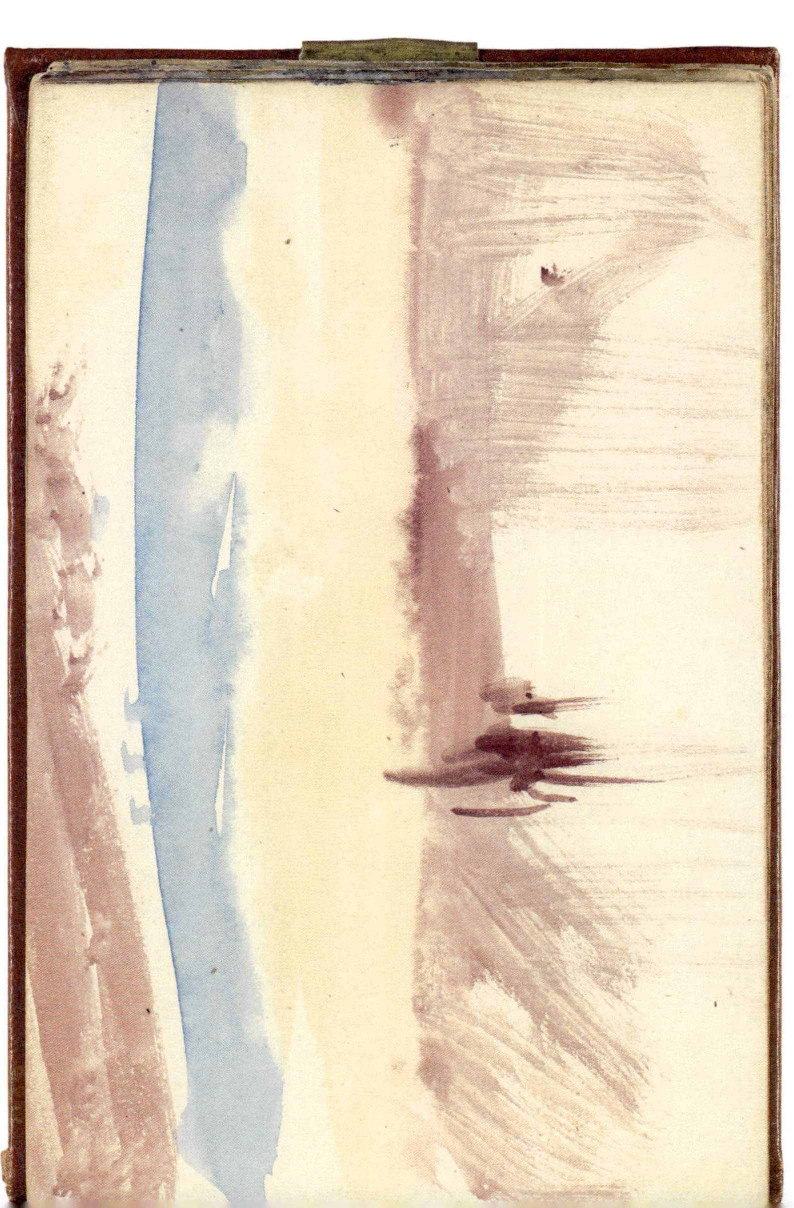

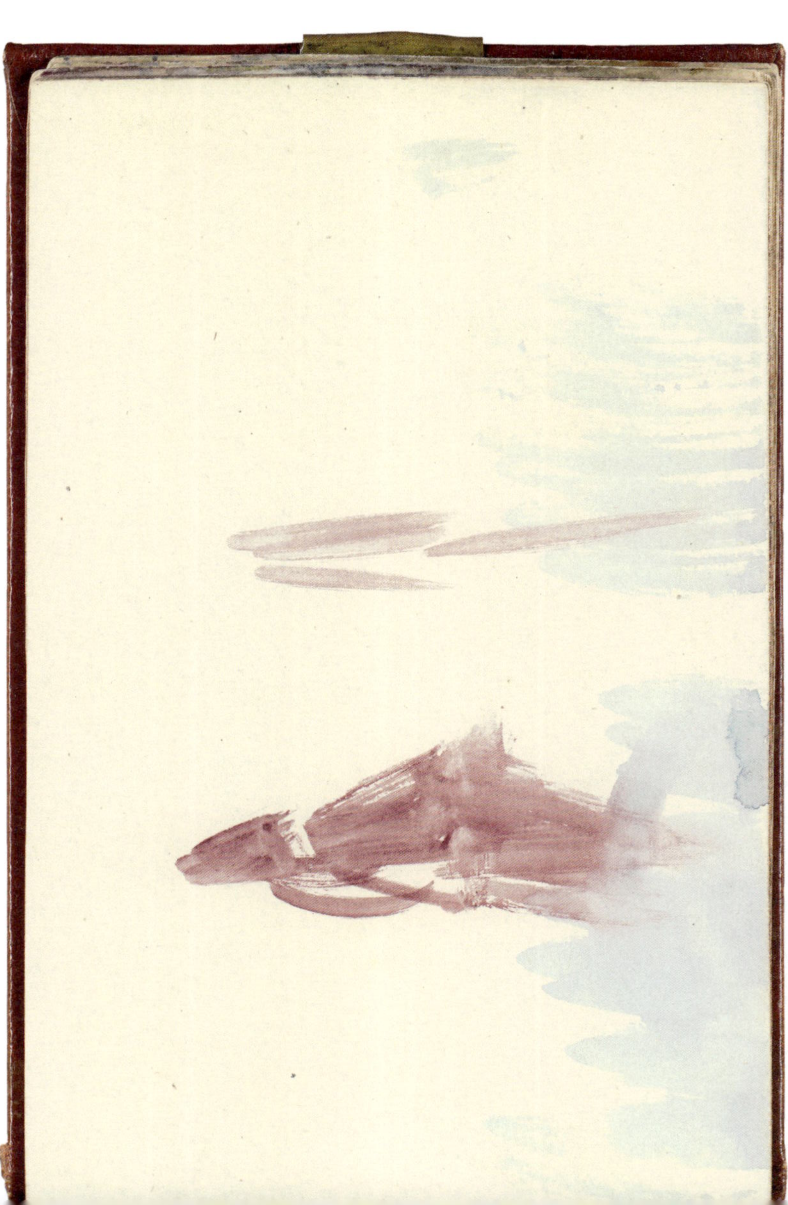

32 V

33 R

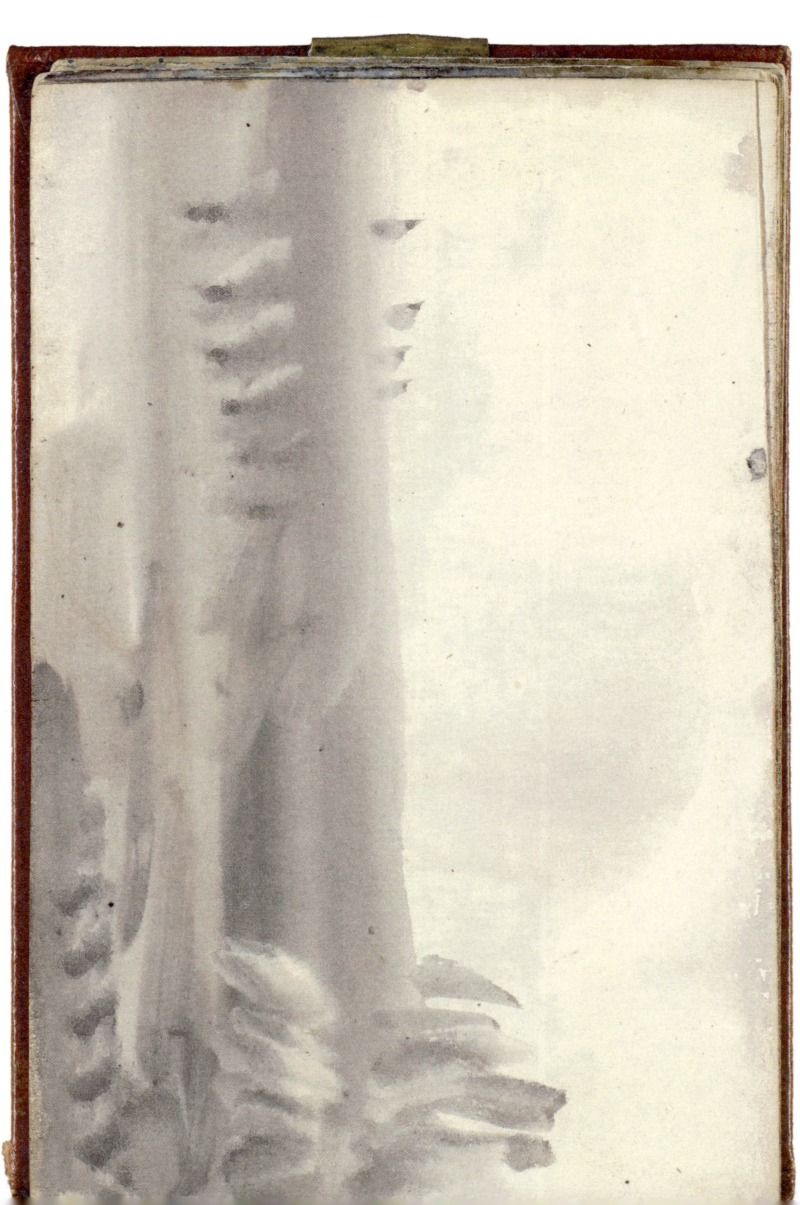

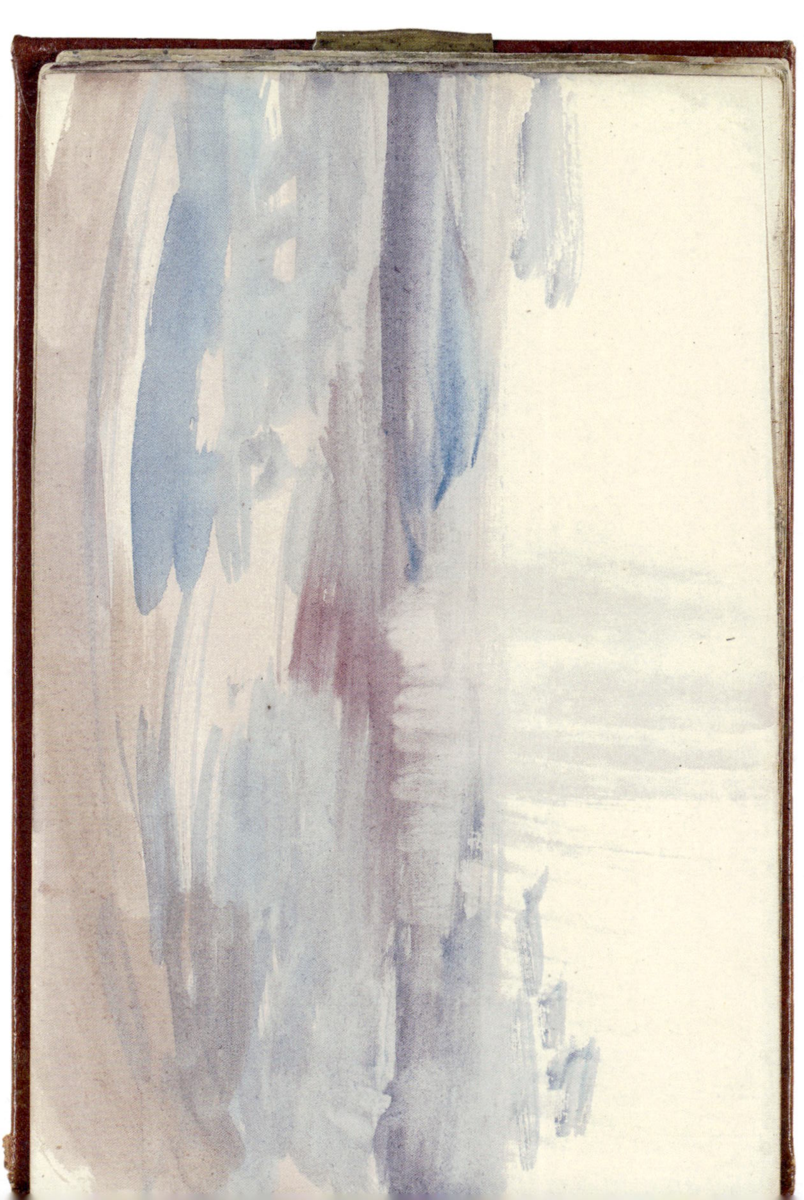

34 v

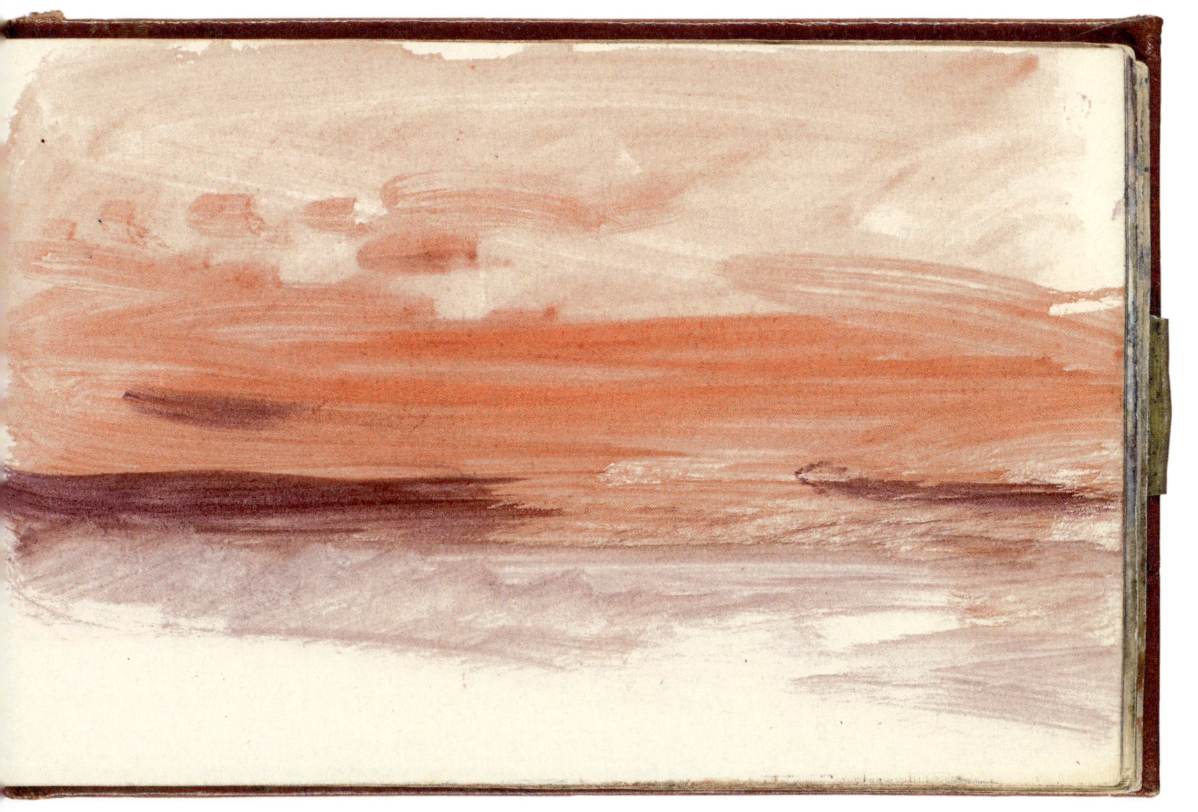

35 R

35 v

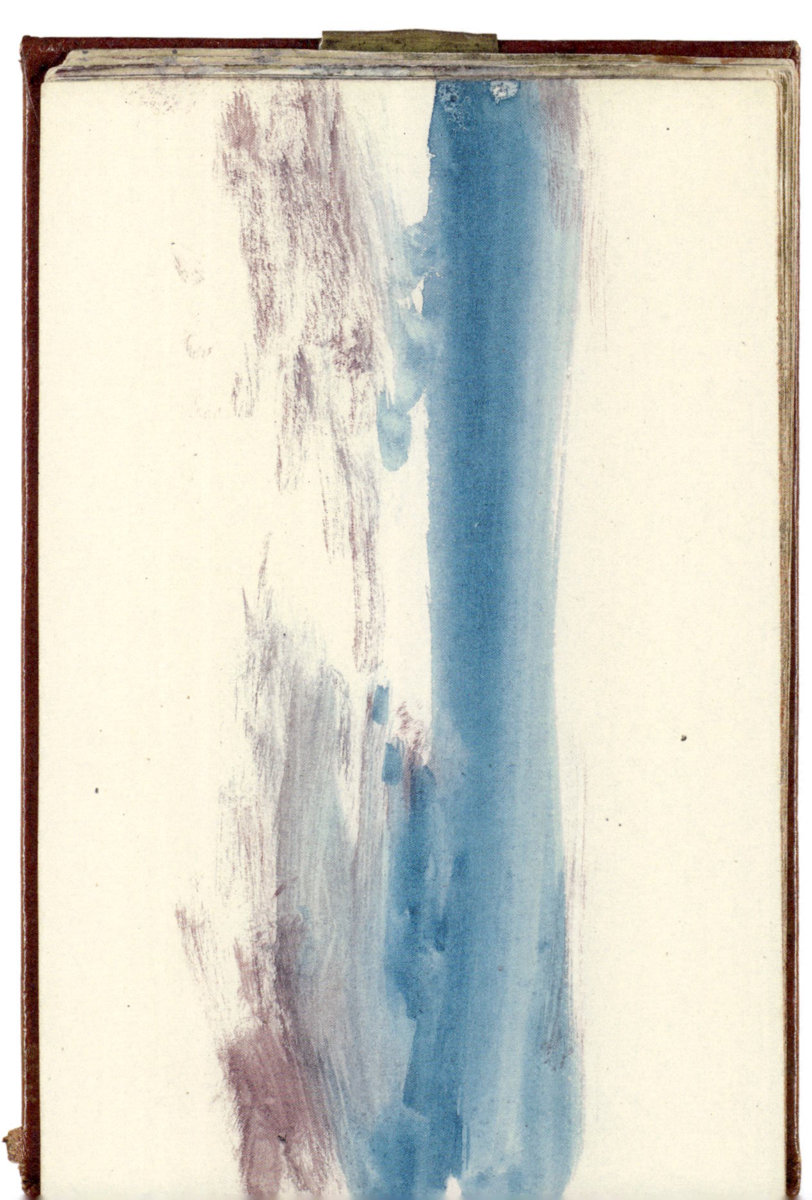

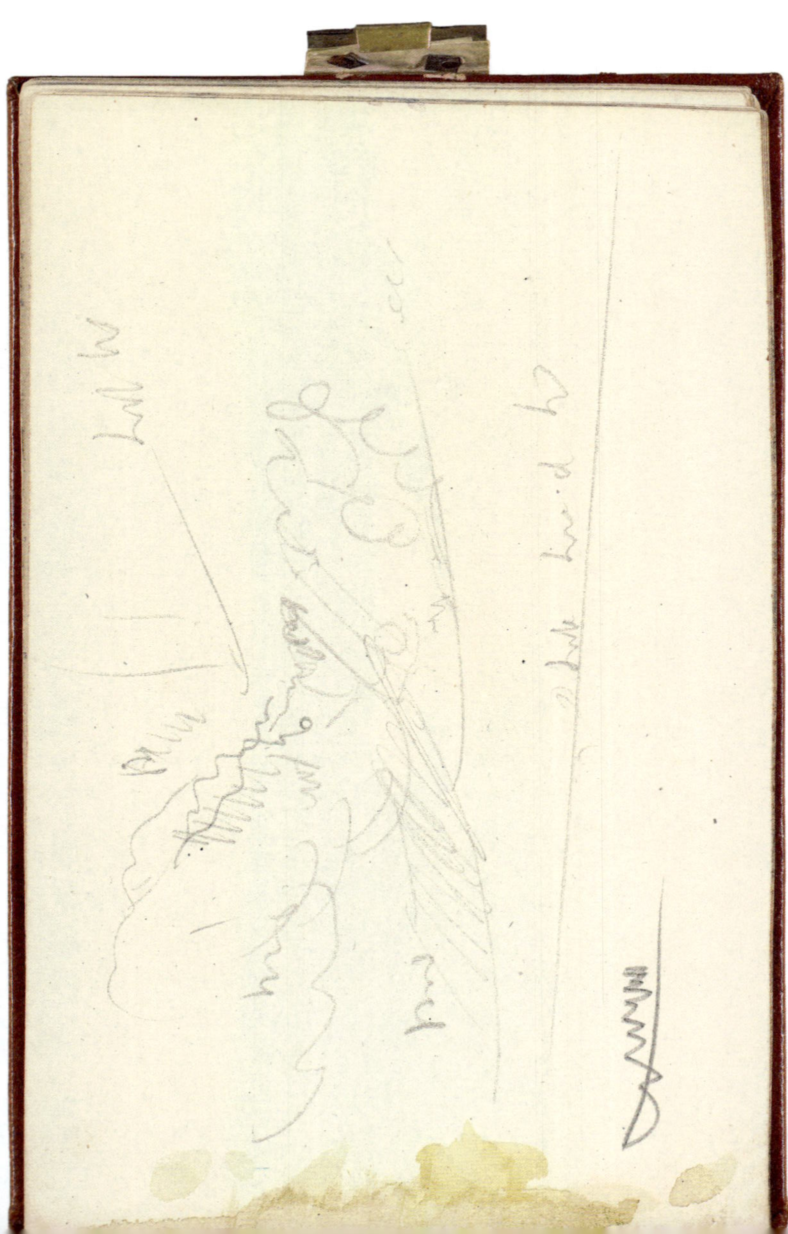

37 R

37 v

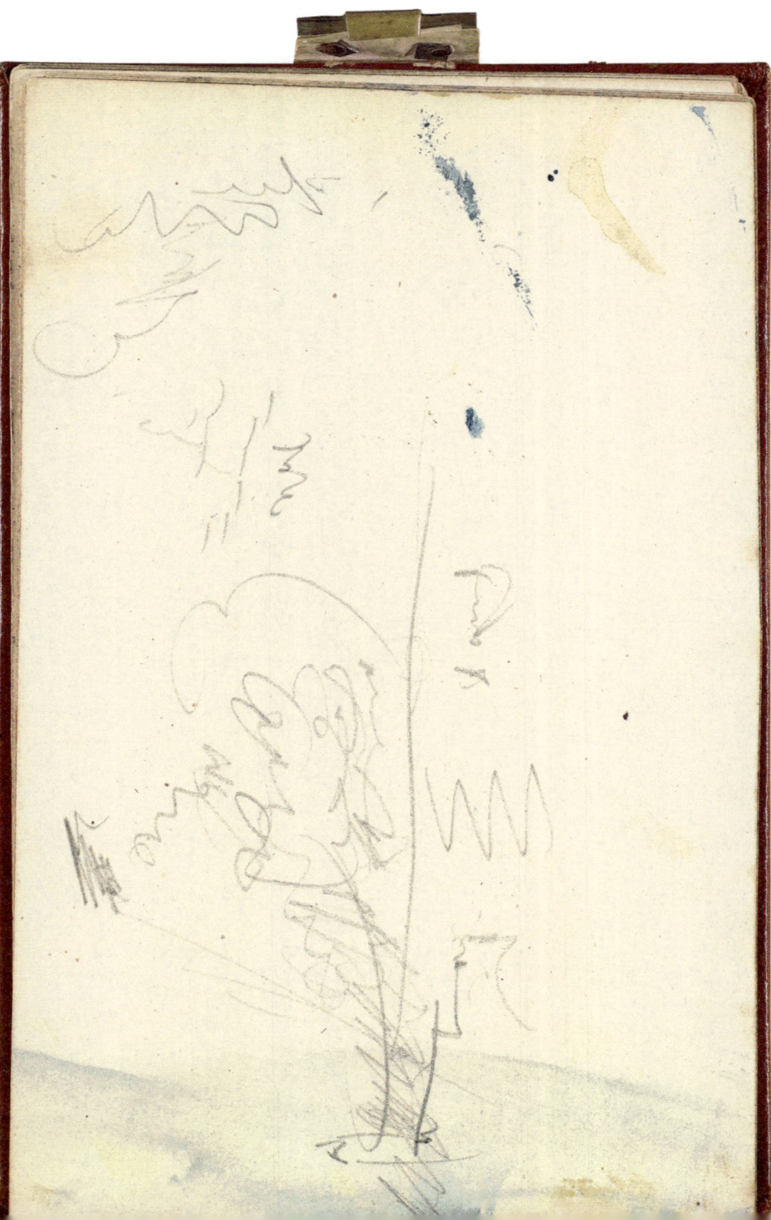

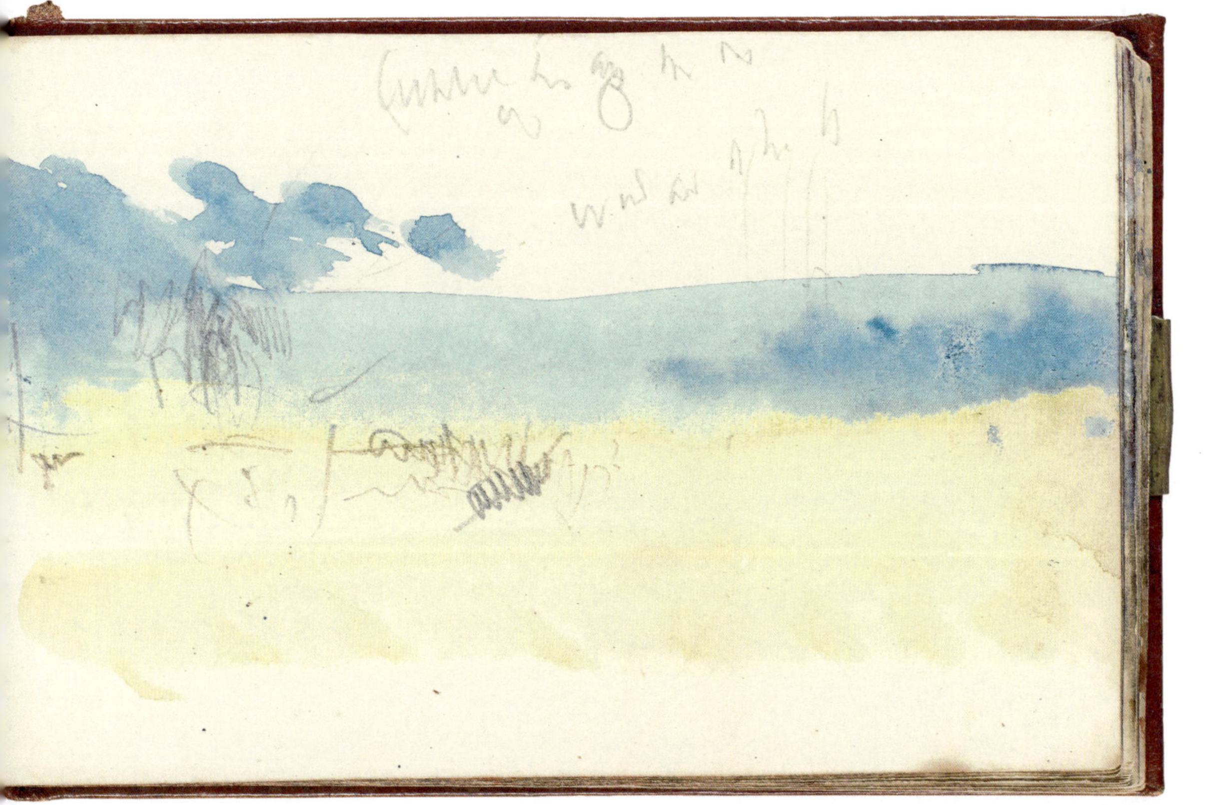

41R

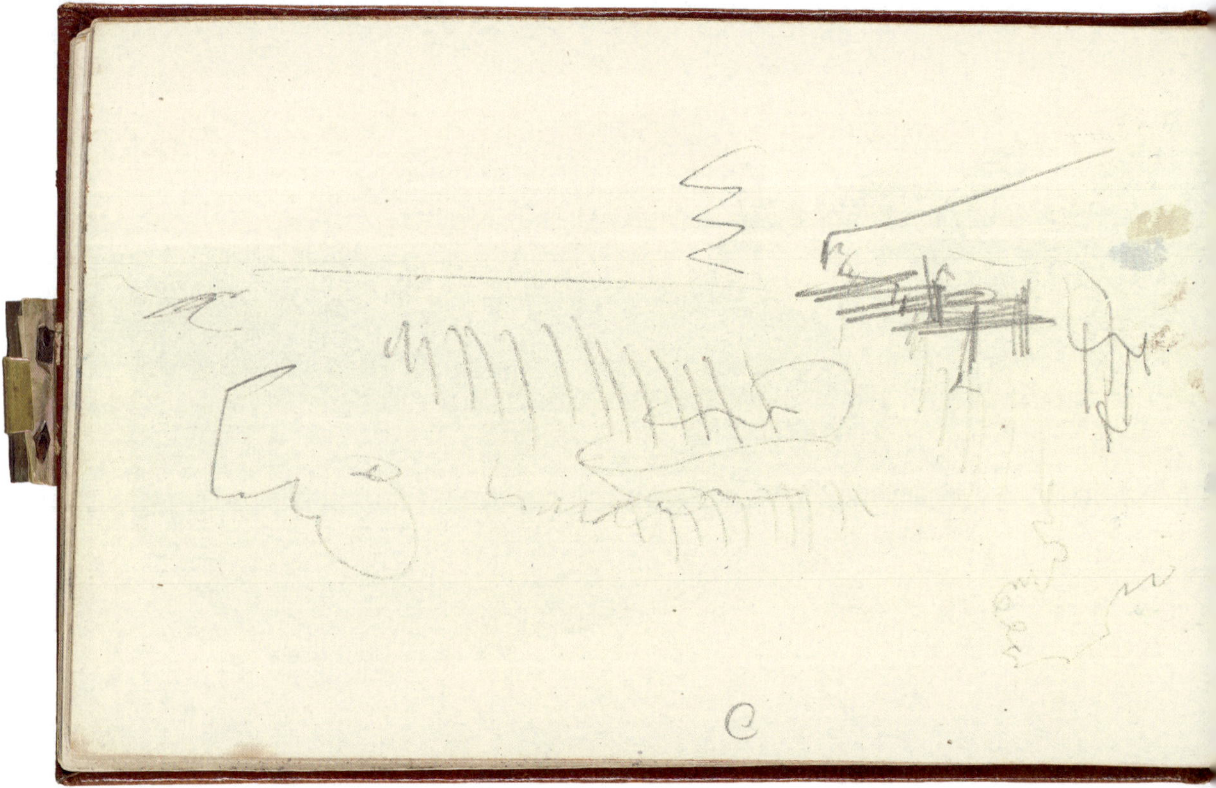

42 v

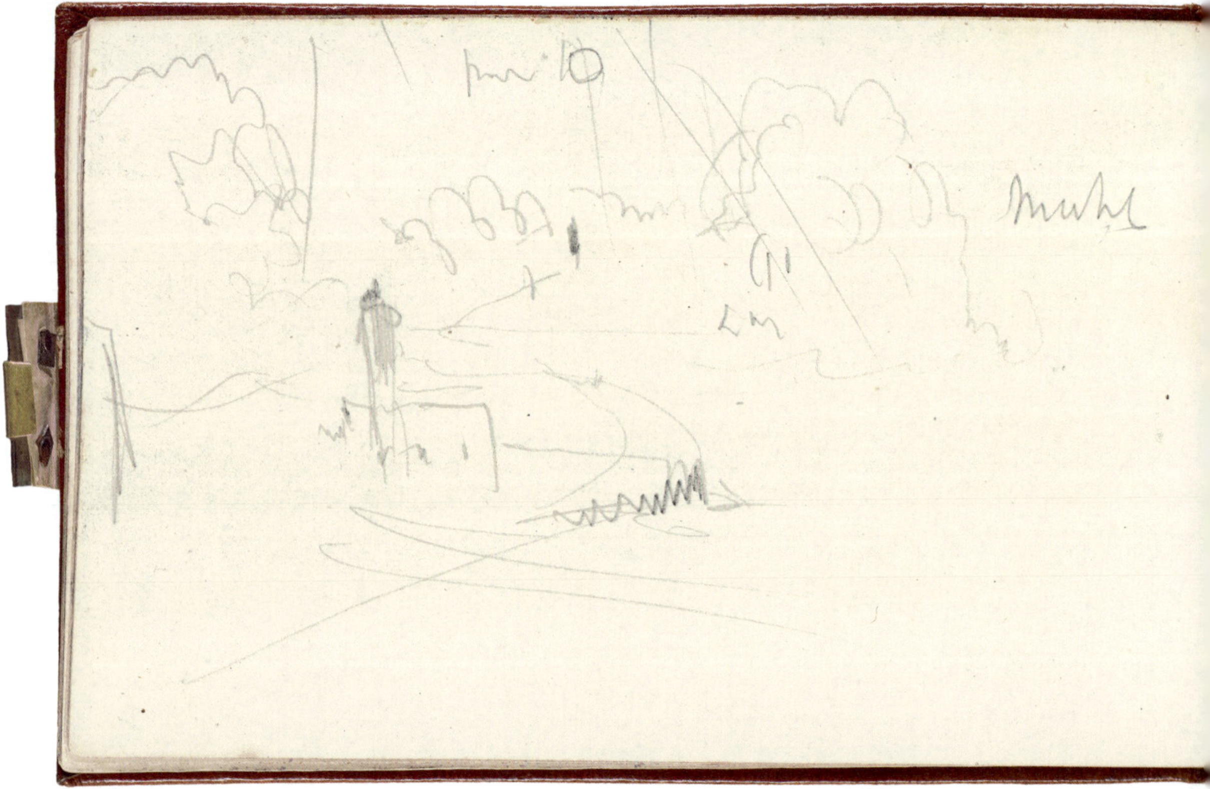

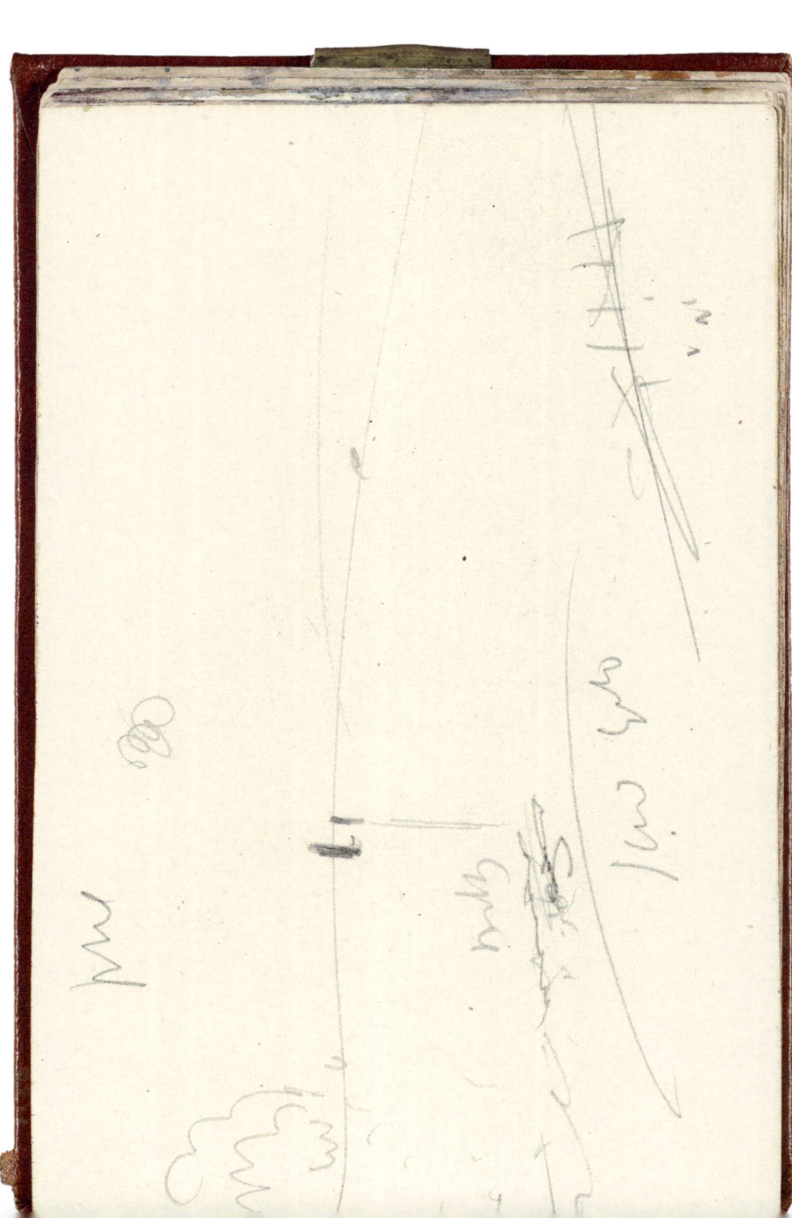

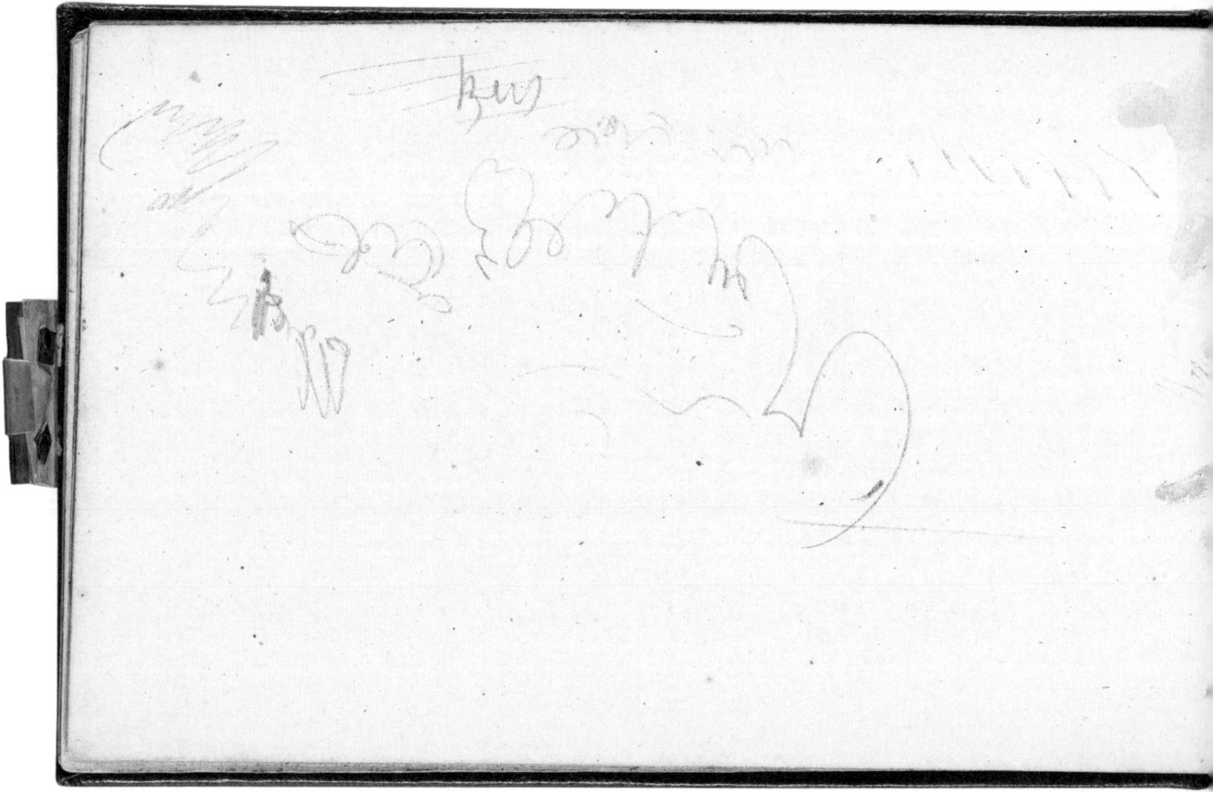

43 v

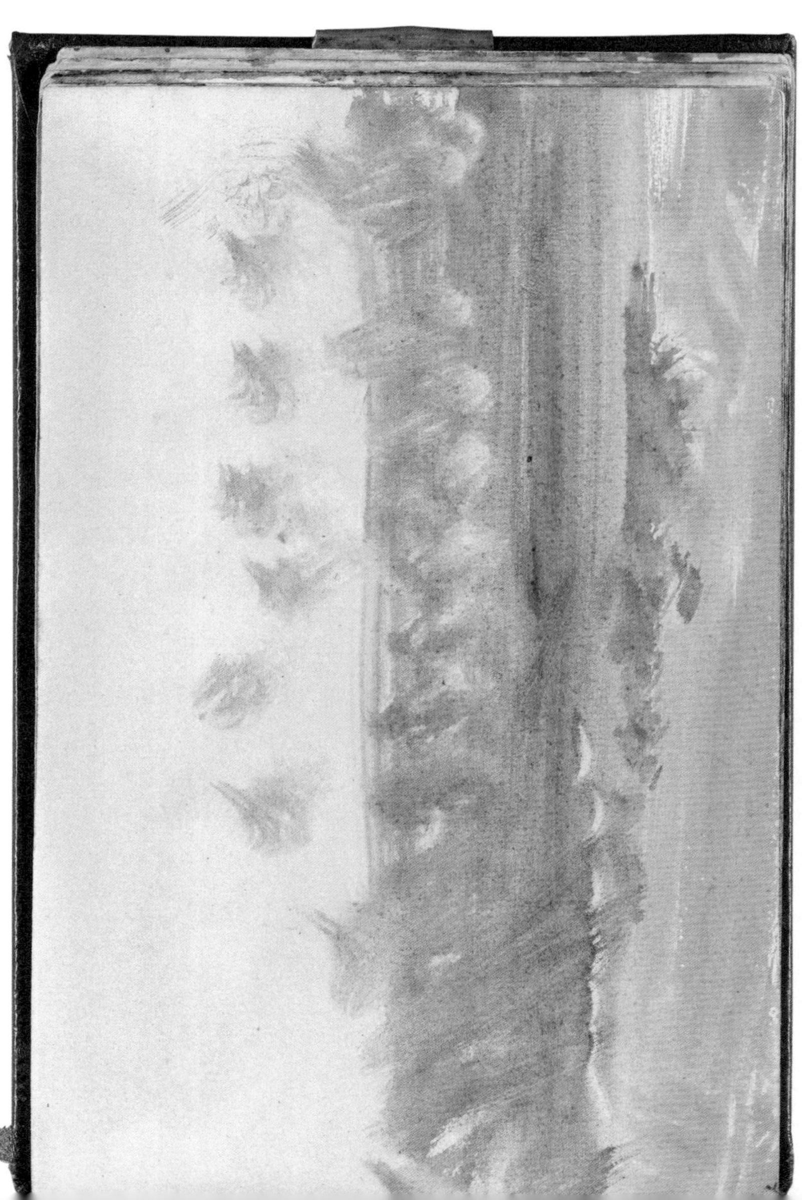

45 R

45 v

47 R

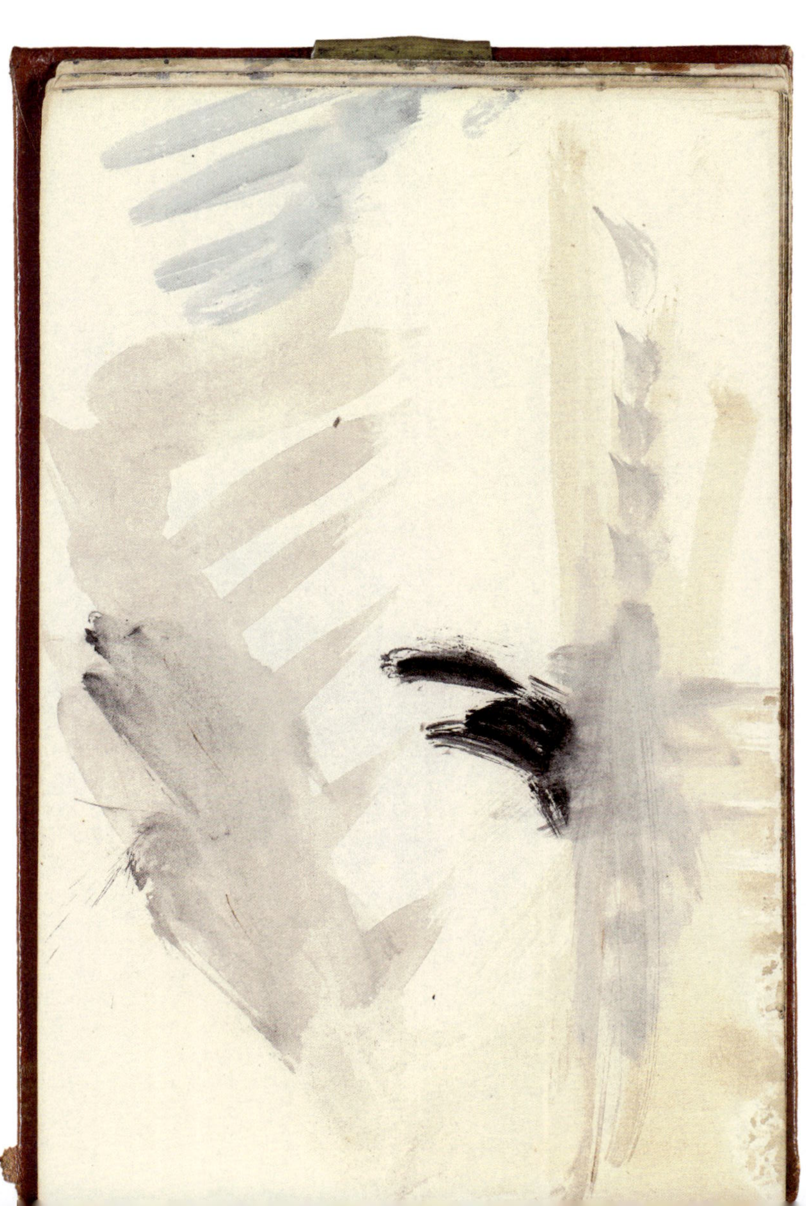

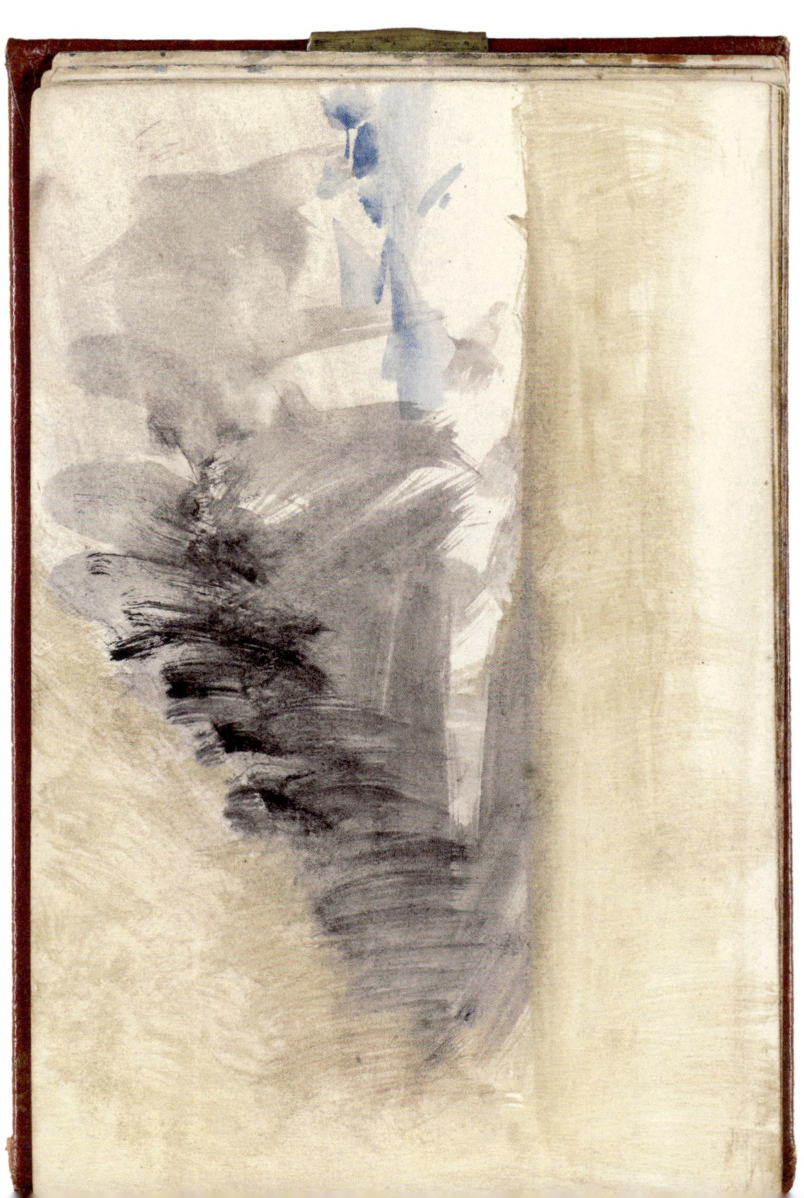

50 R

52 R

52 v

53 v

54 R

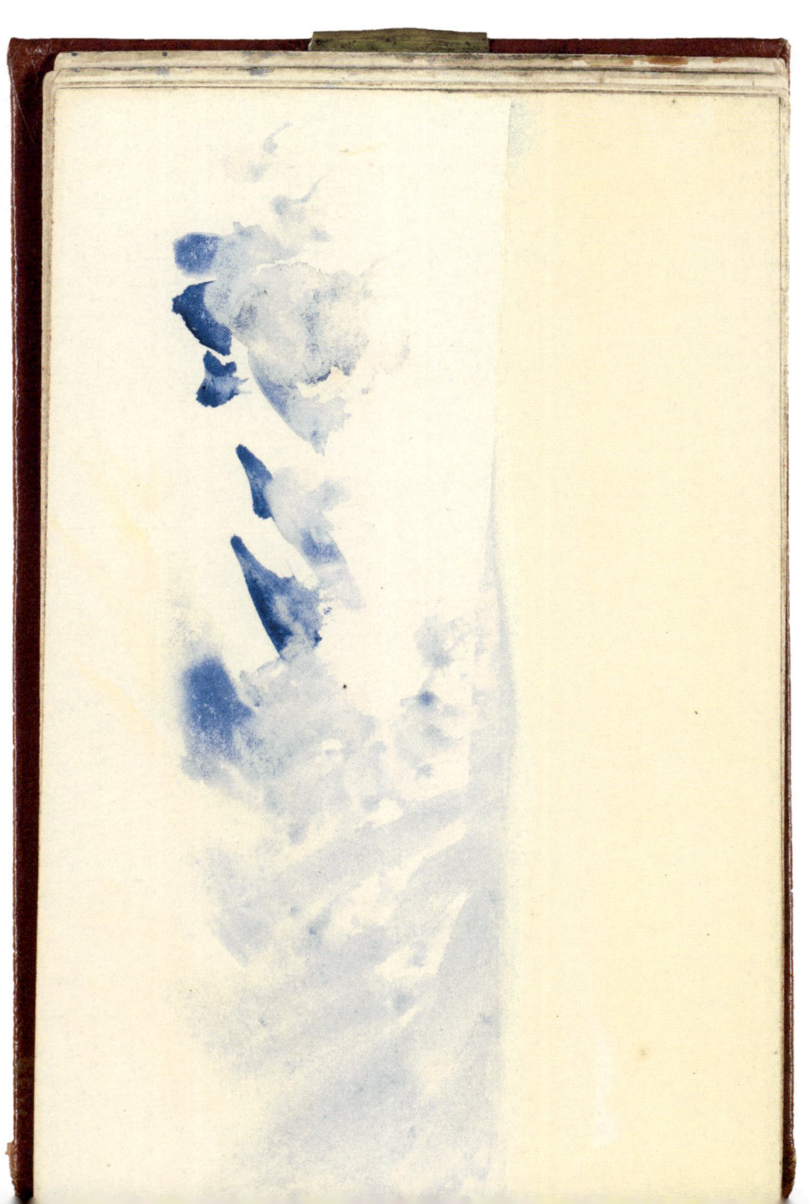

57R

58R

59 R

60 R

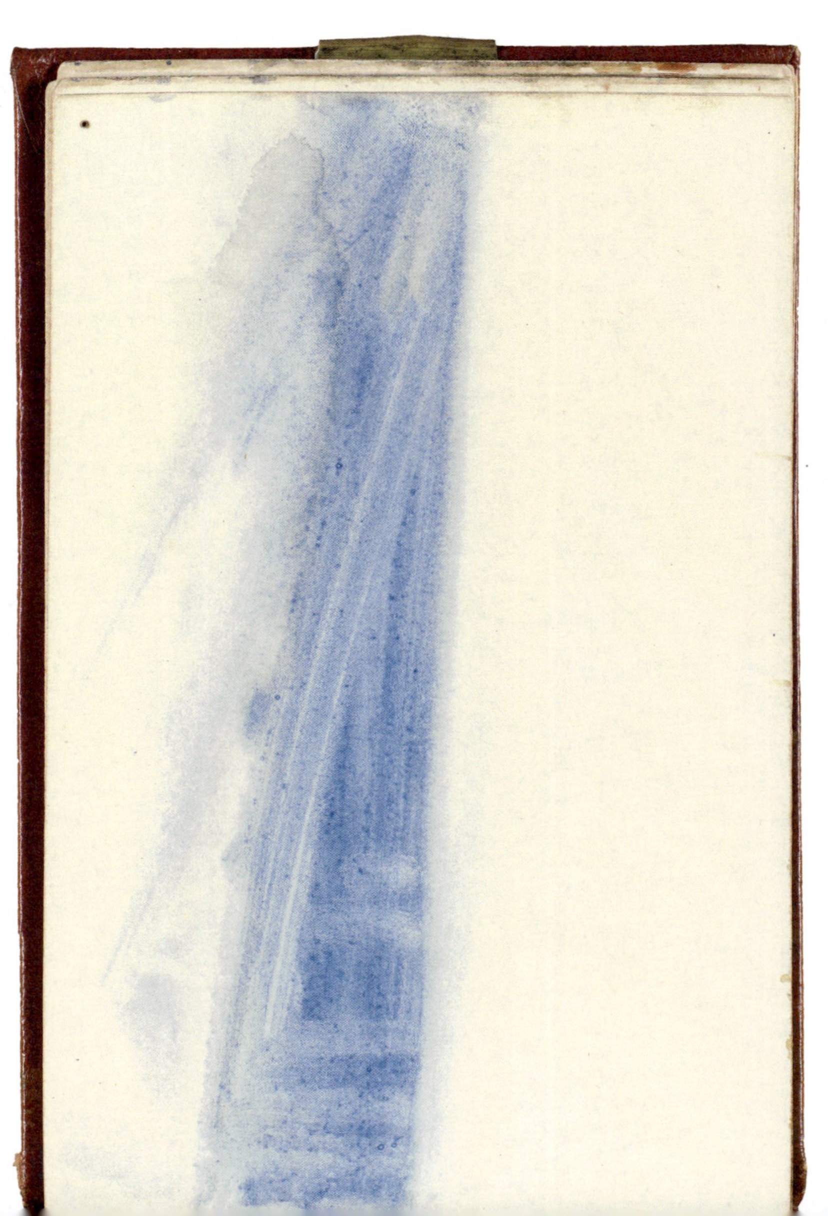

63 R

64 v

65 R

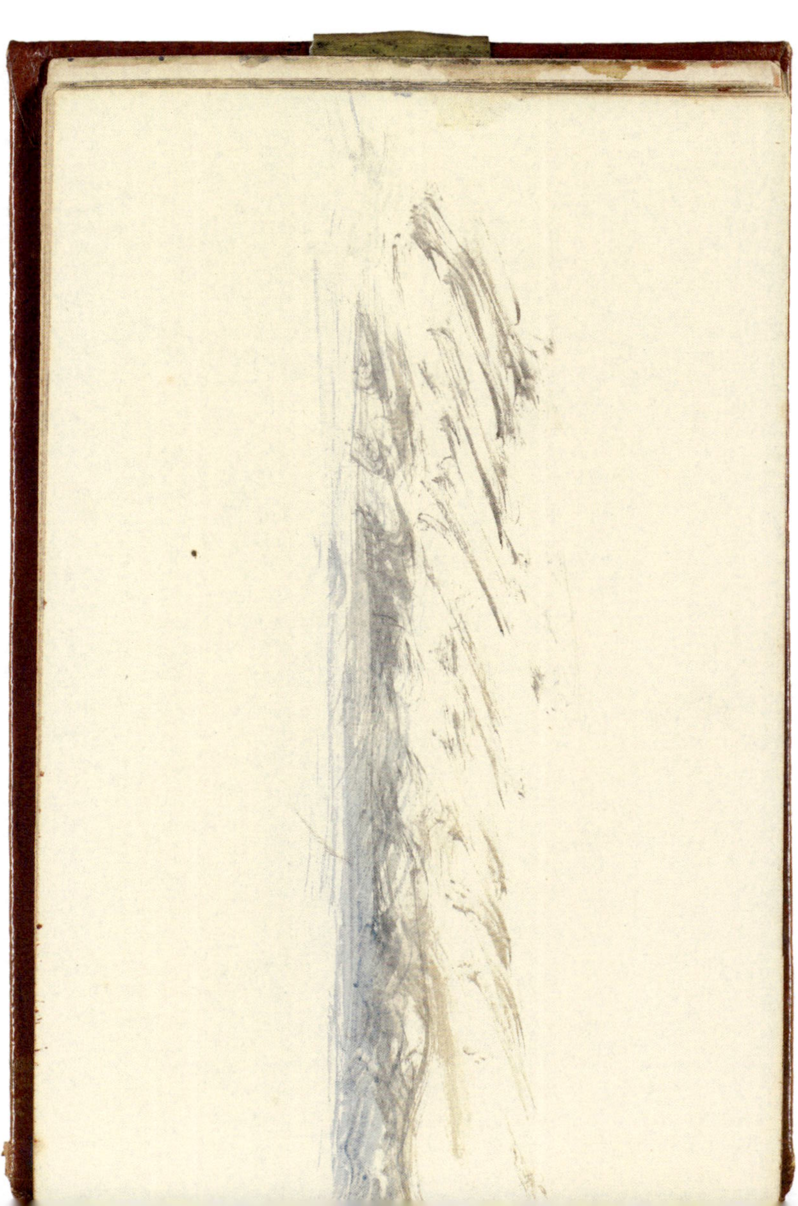

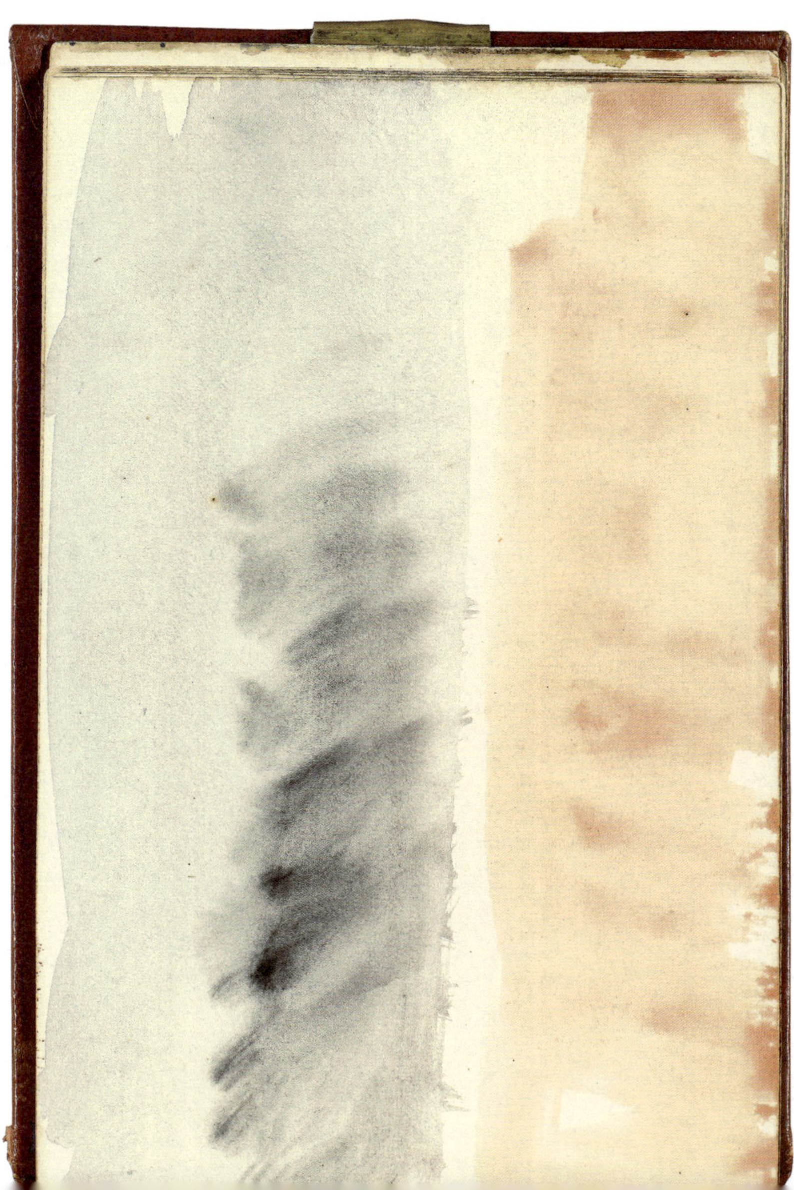

67v

69 v

20

70 v

61

71 v

72 R

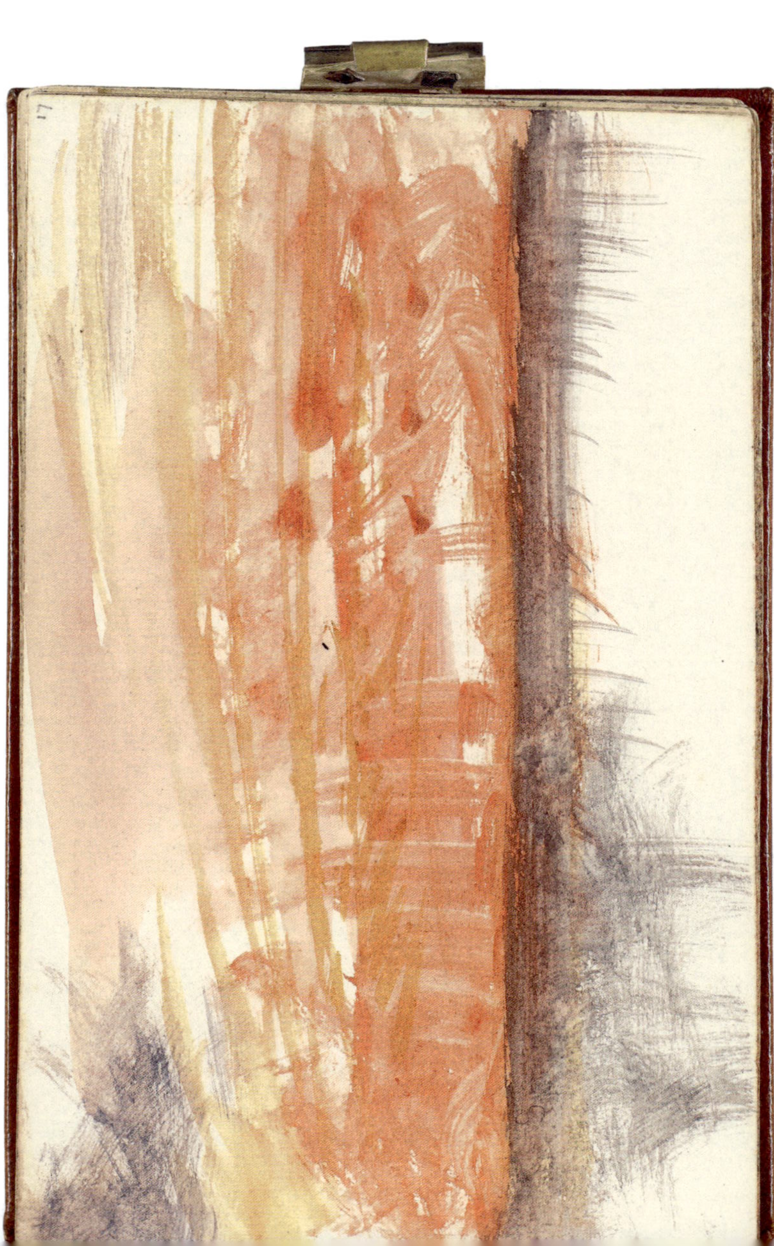

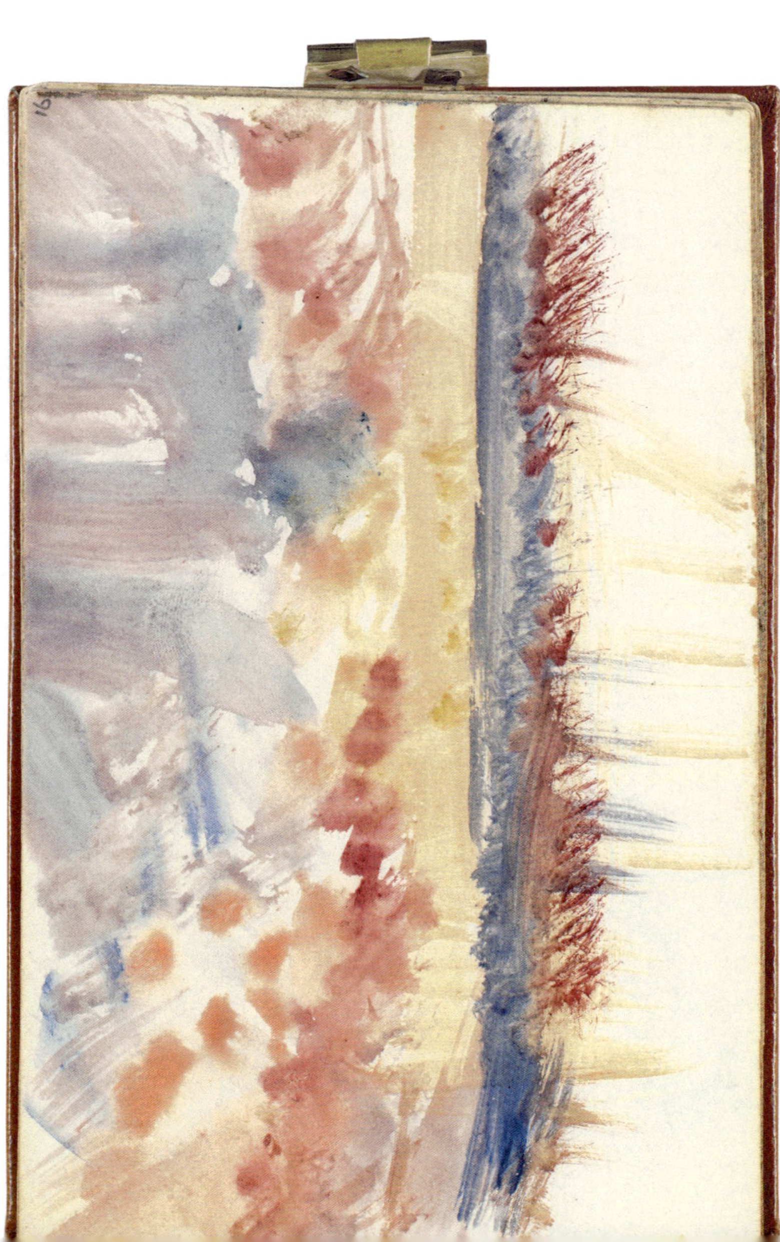

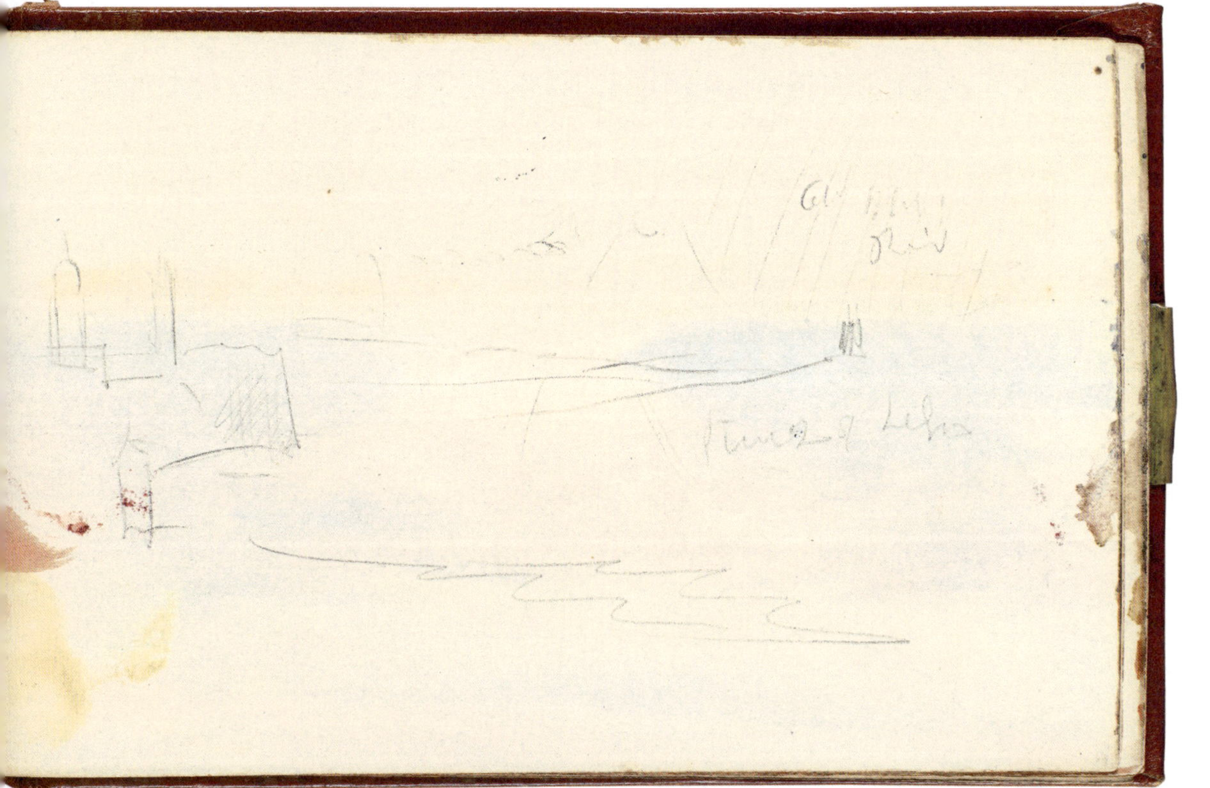

74 R

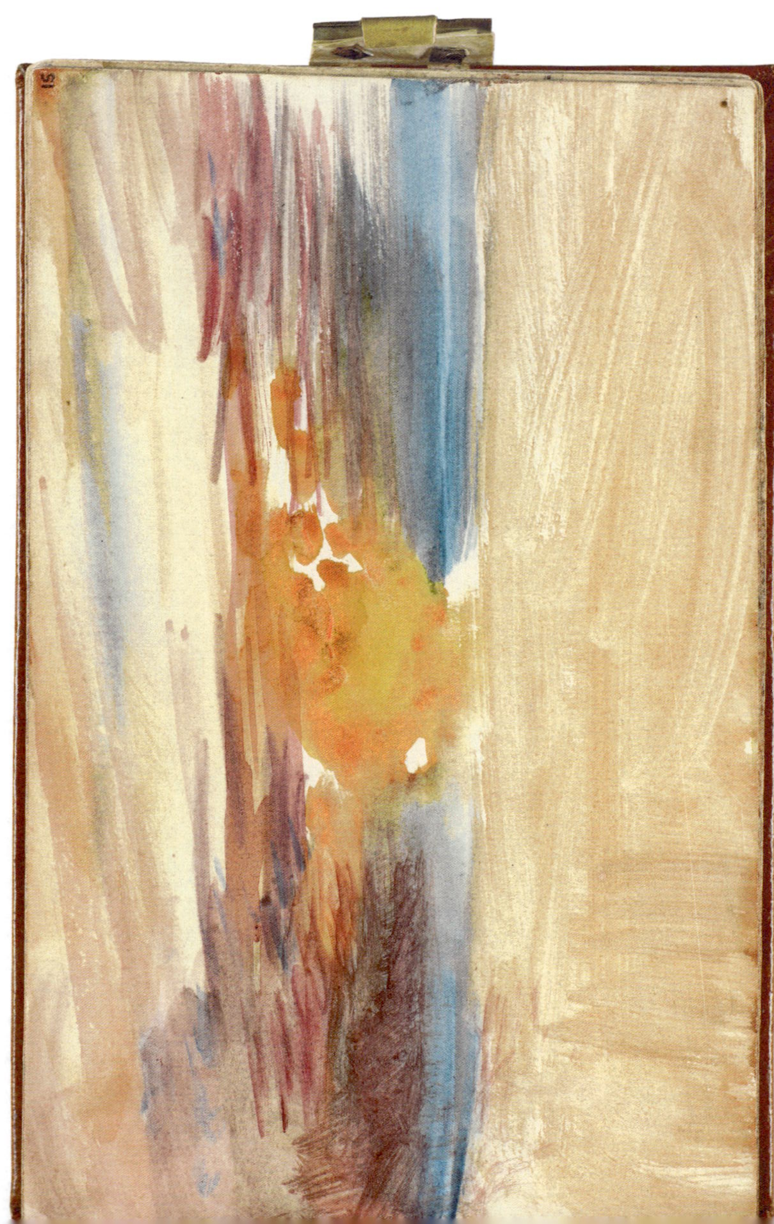

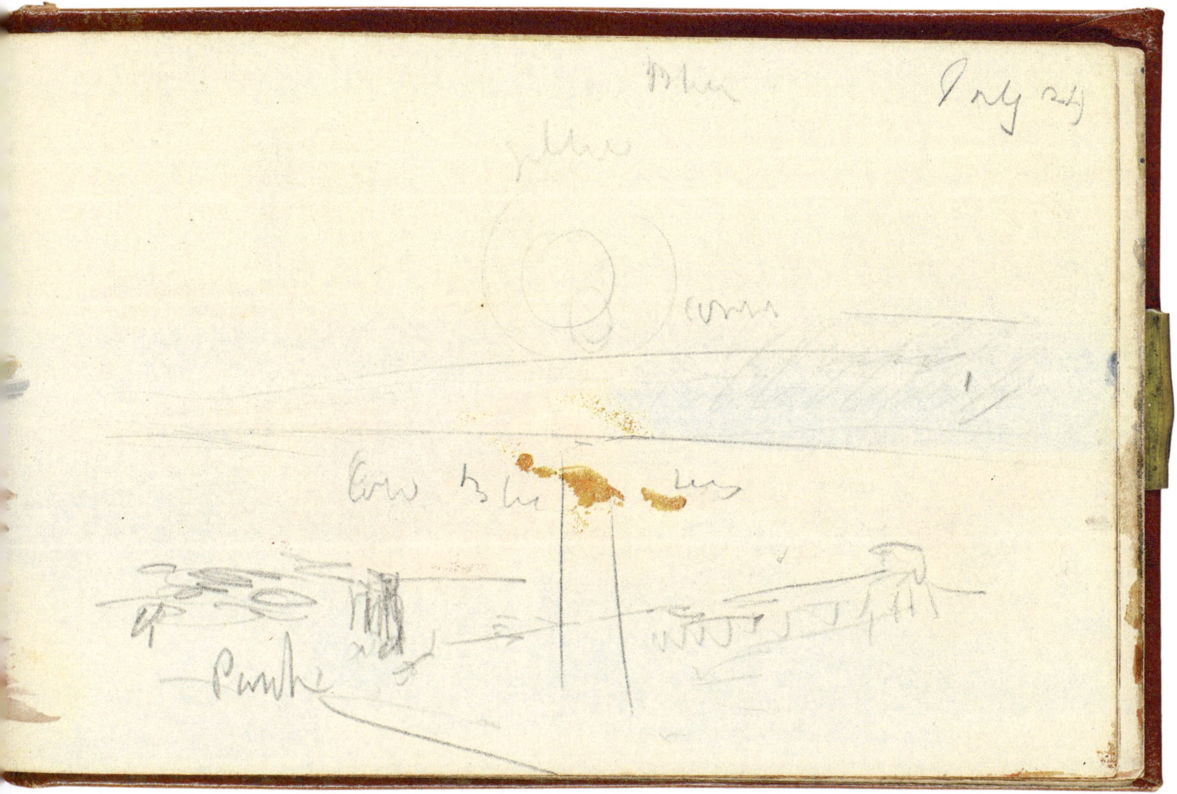

75 R

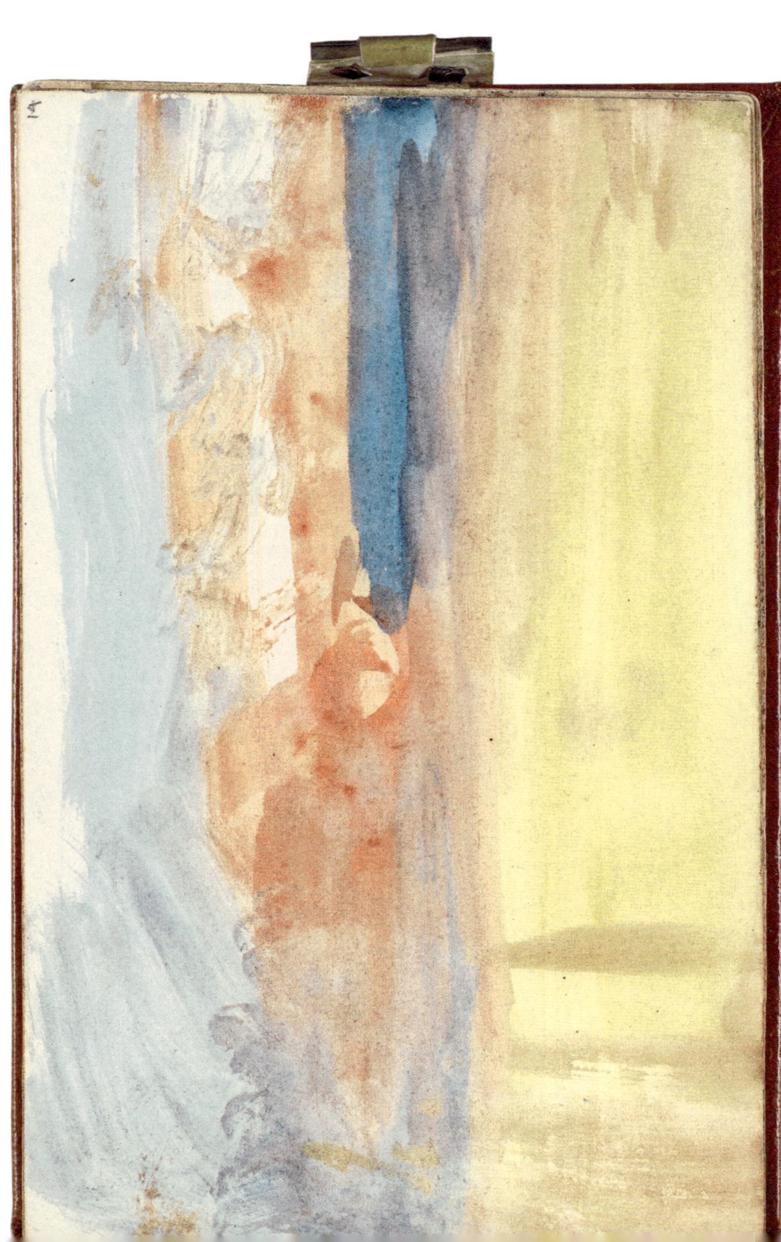

76 R

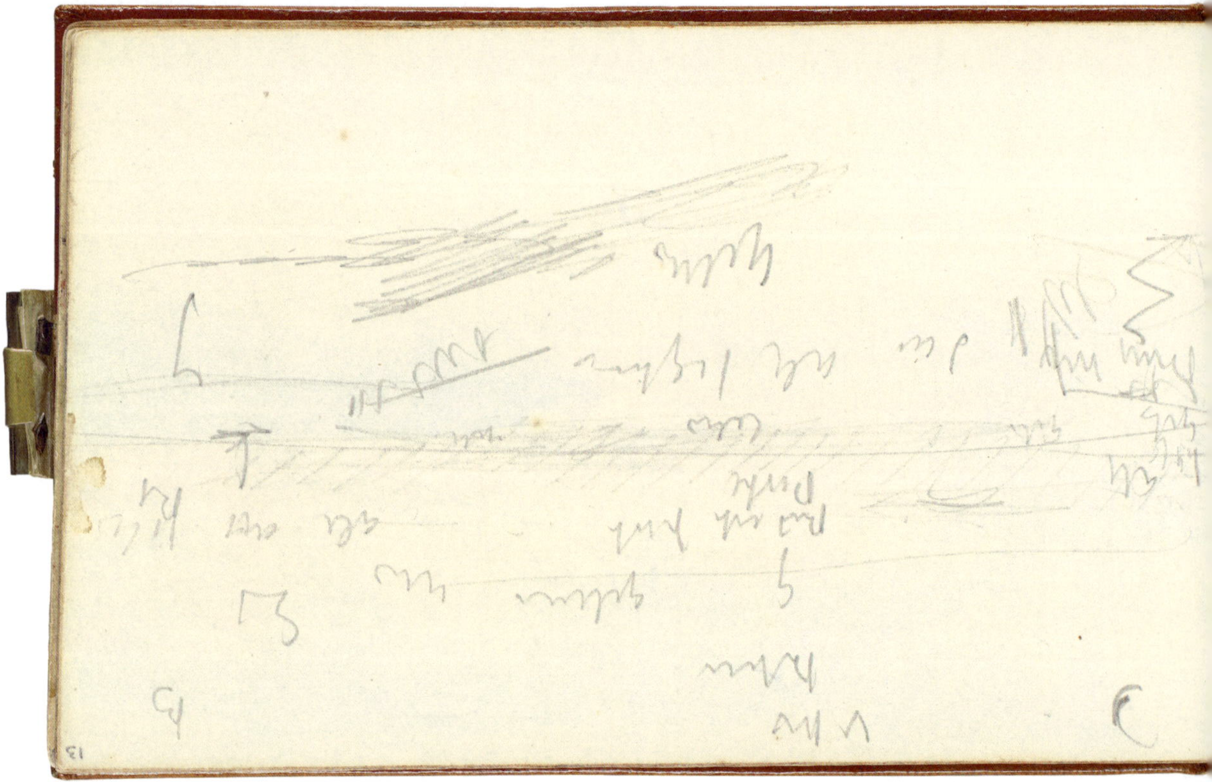

12

The lowest part with water Dull [illegible]
& the sea going the other [illegible] the Haze
sheets

77v

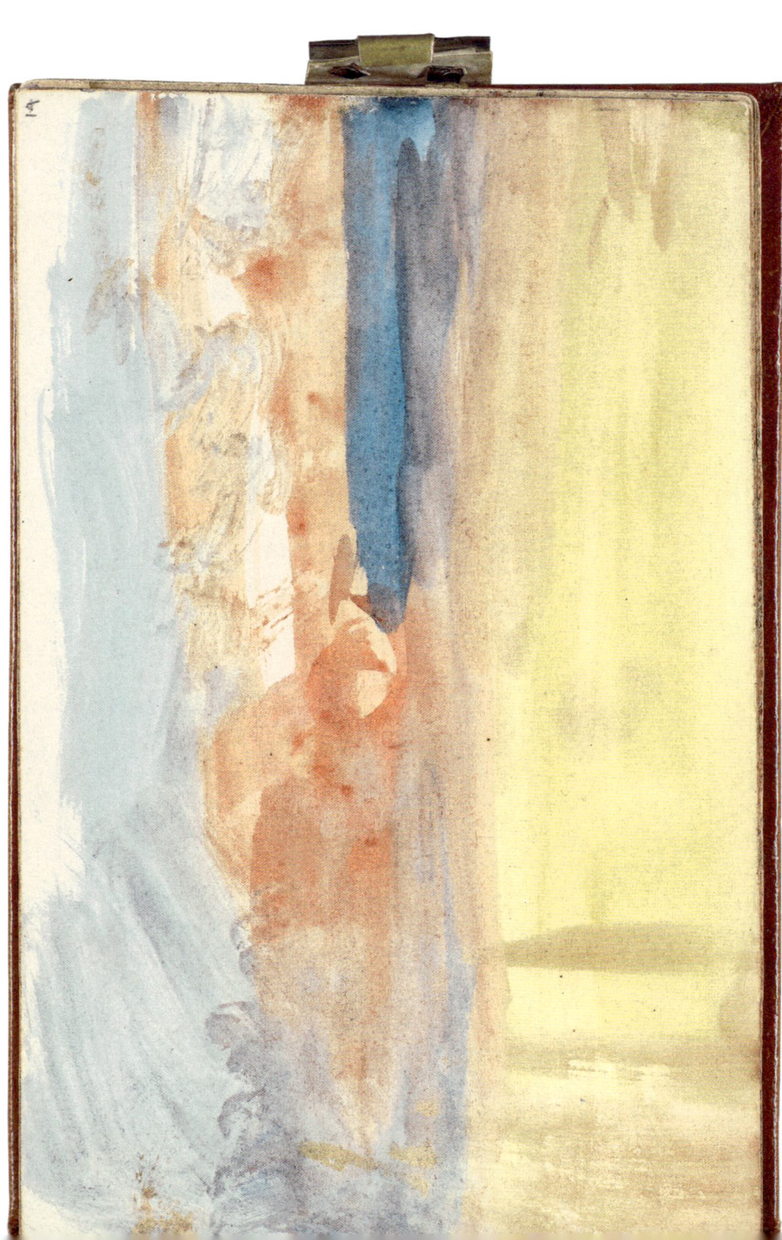

76 R

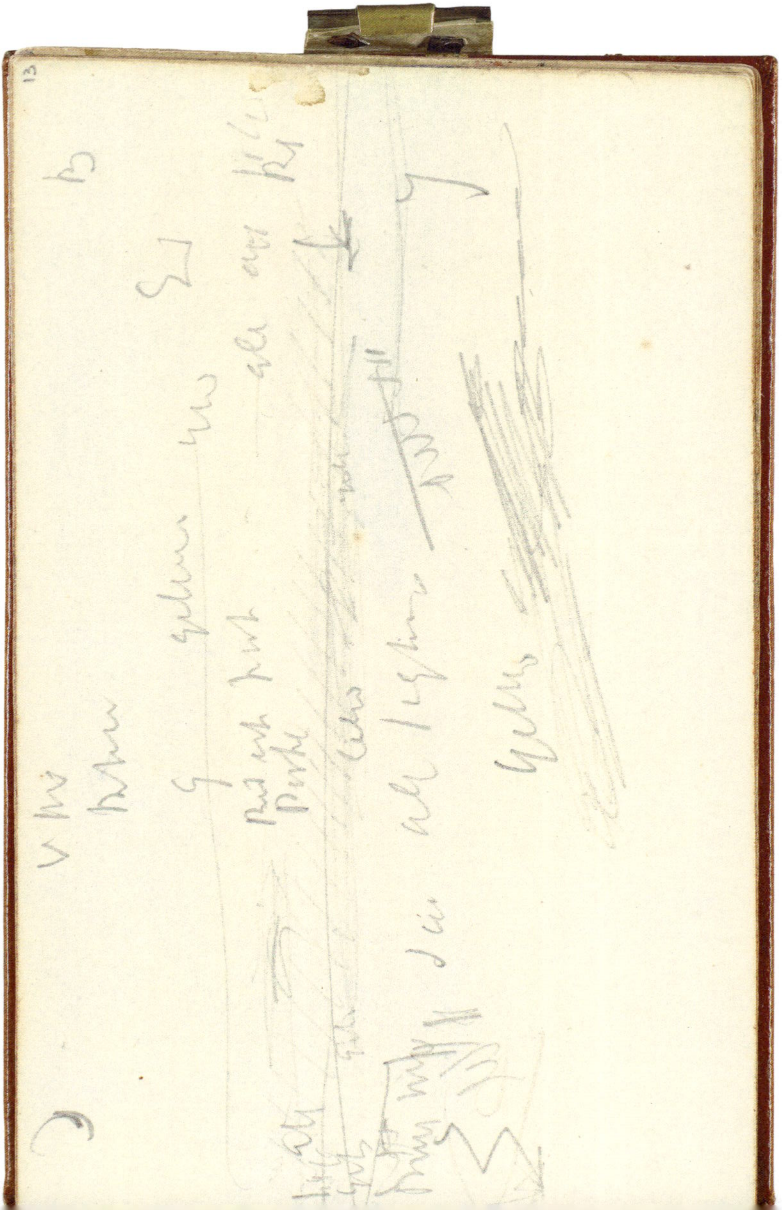

76 v

12

77v

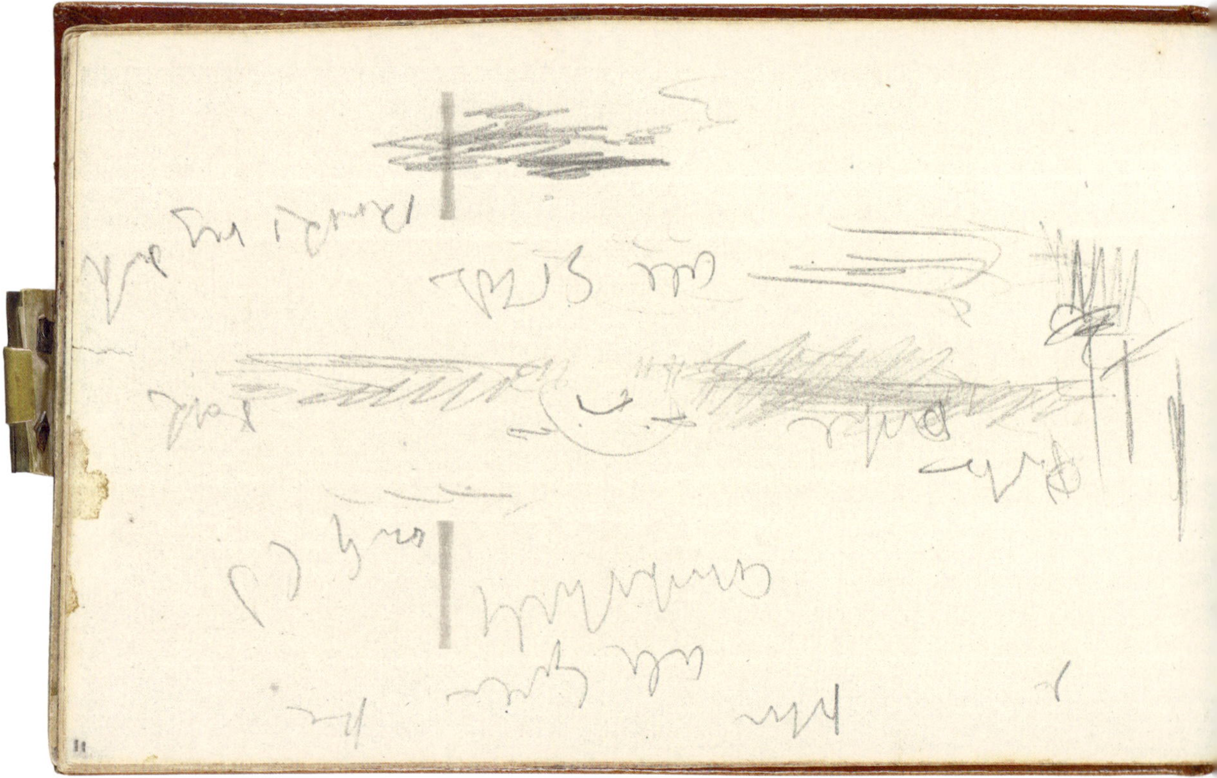

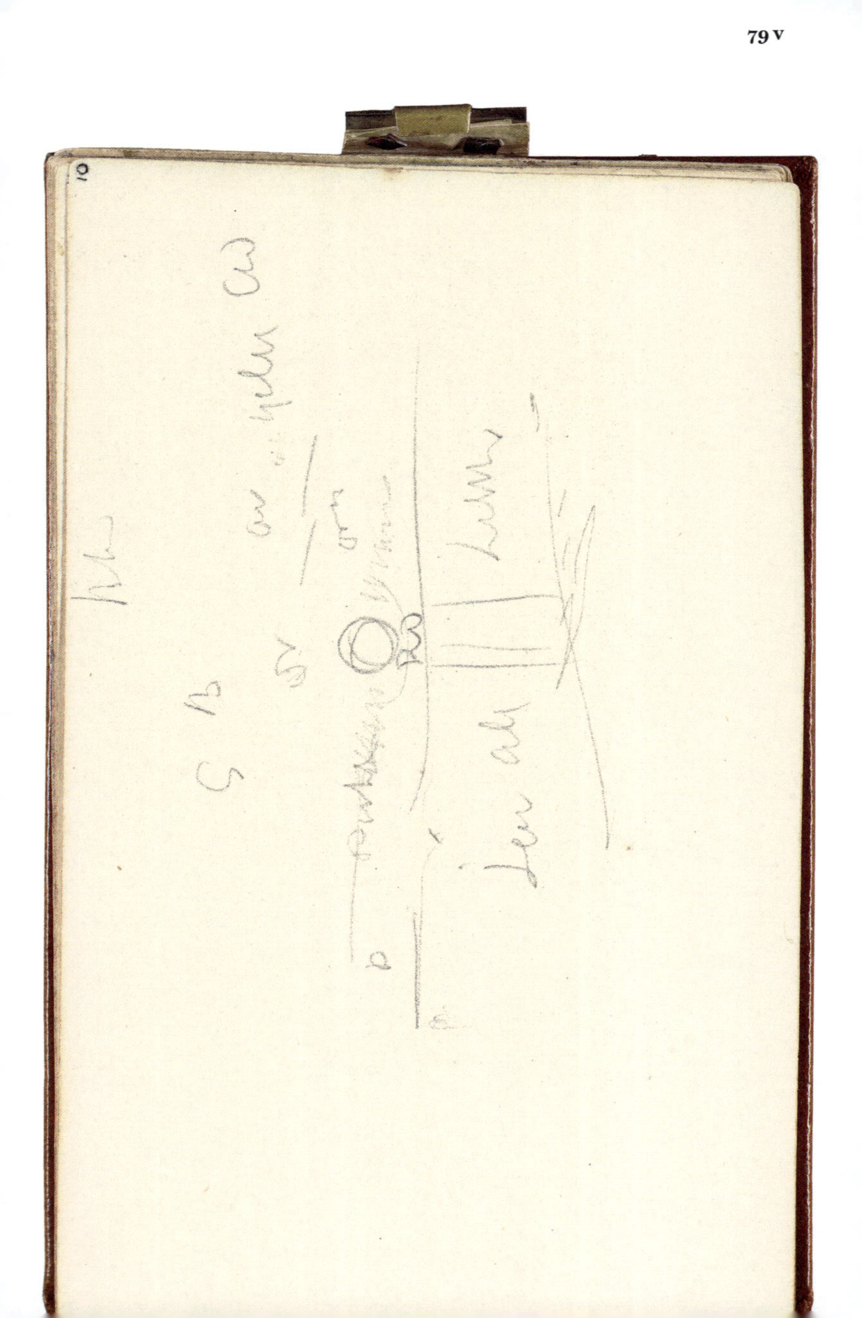

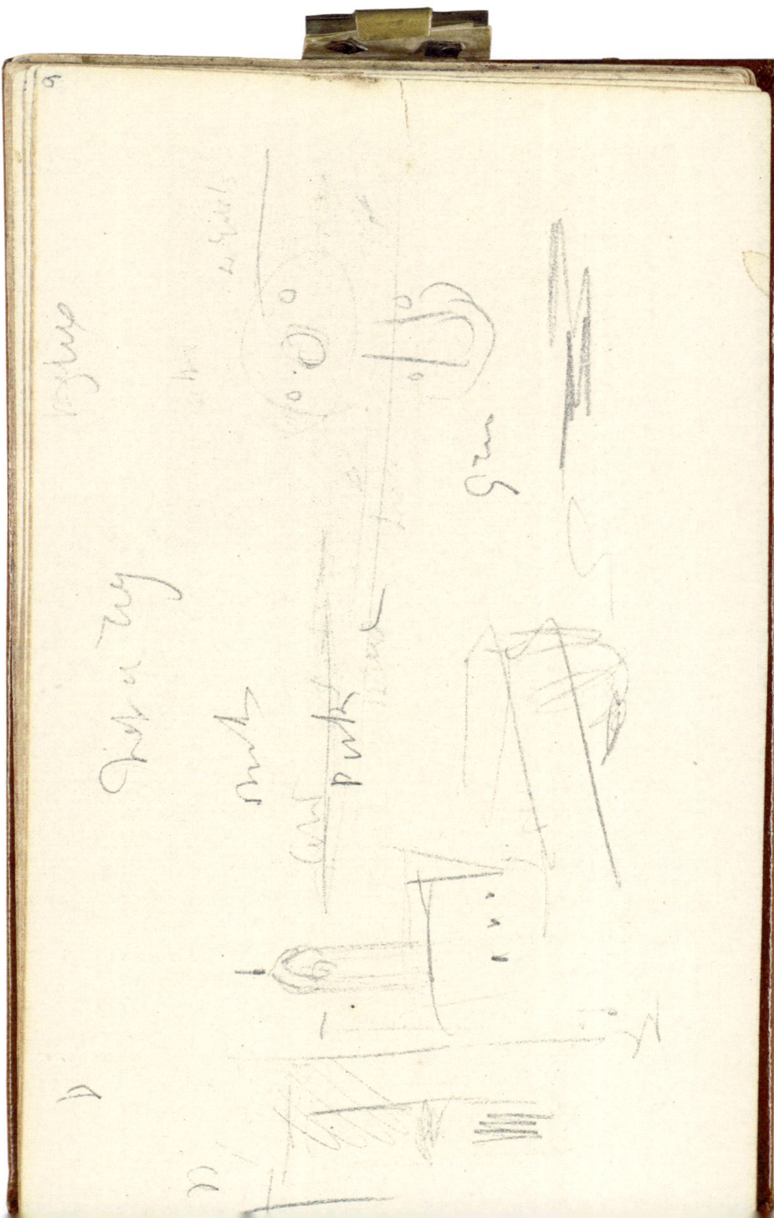

81 v

82R

82 v

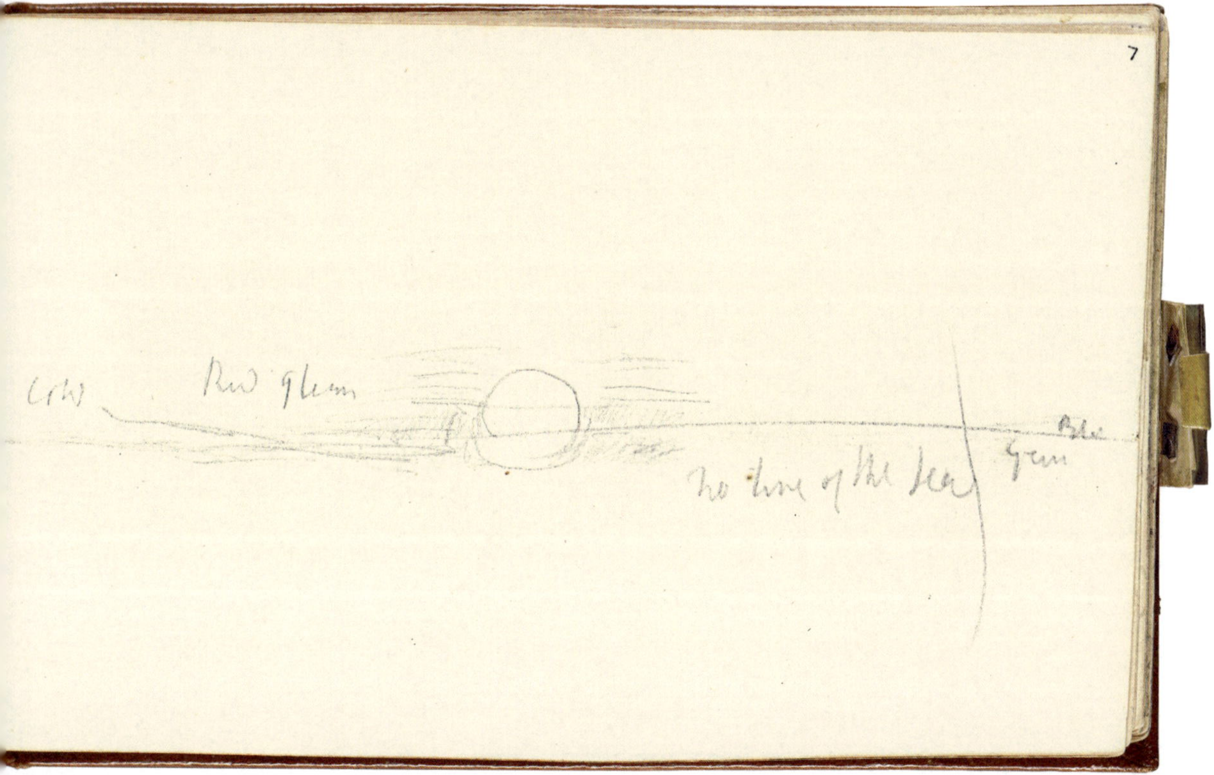

7

Cold

Red gleam

No line of the sea

Green

Blue

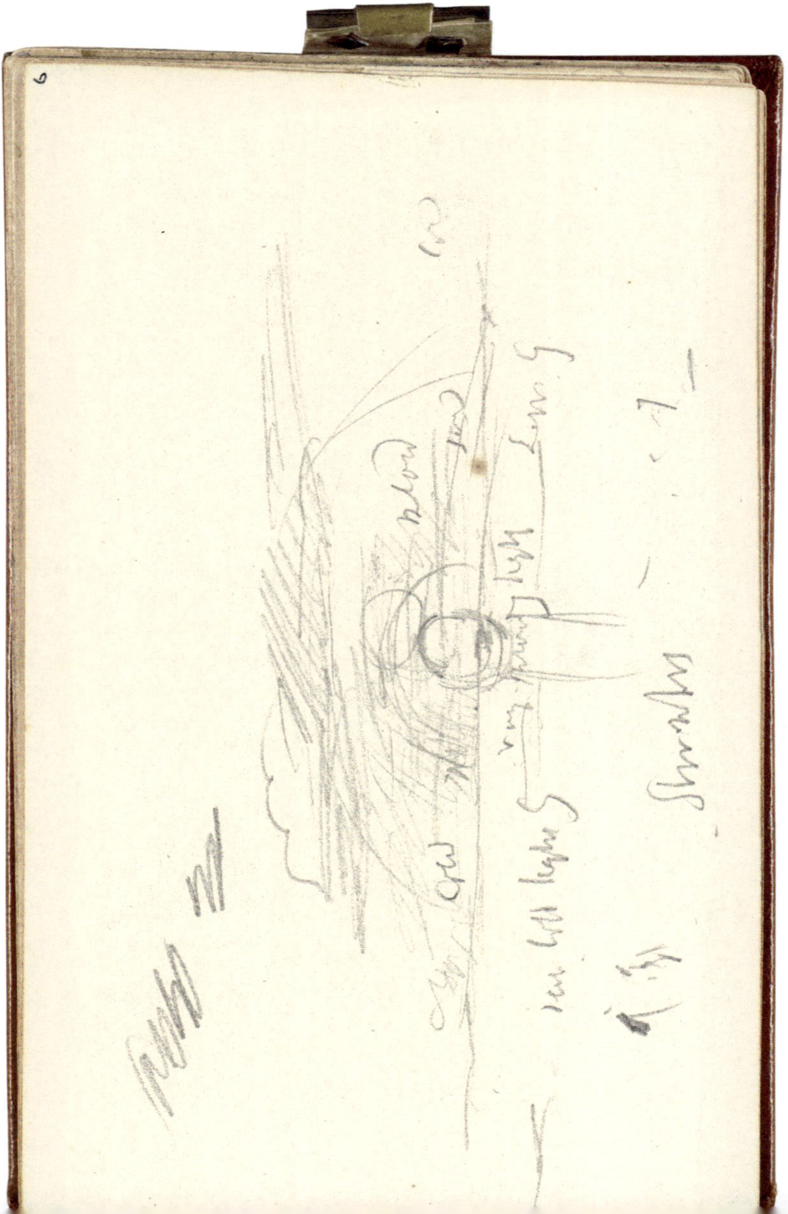

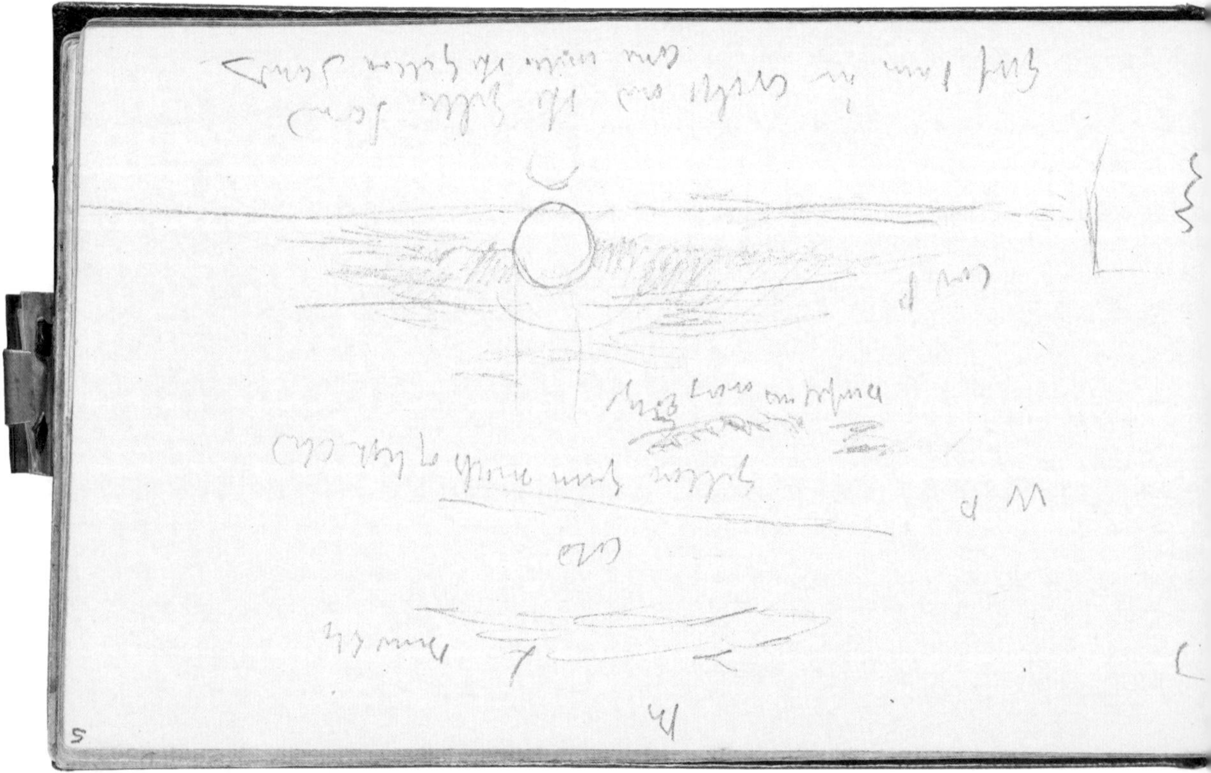

84 v

5

cold

W P

yellow green mists of light cloud

cool P

Gulf I am in circles and the golden sand
come unto the yellow sands

85 v

A 98 v

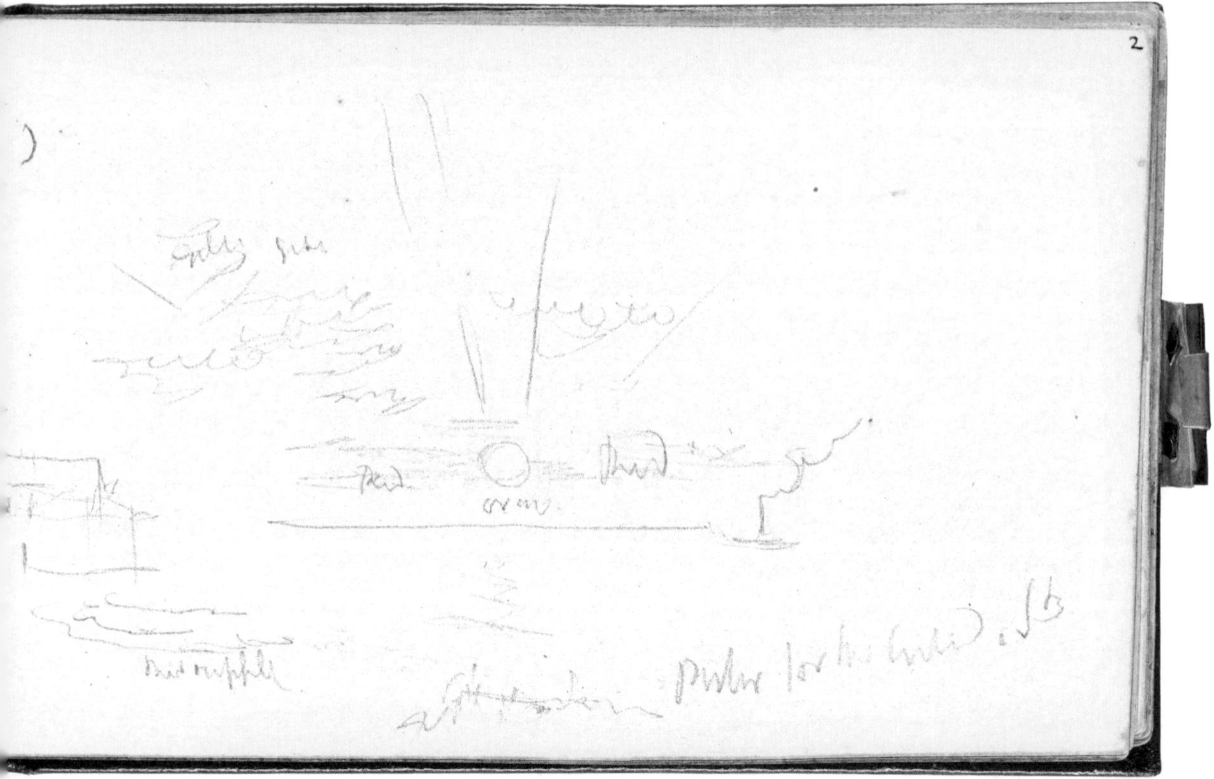

2

88v

blue

Red

[illegible]

[illegible]

[illegible]

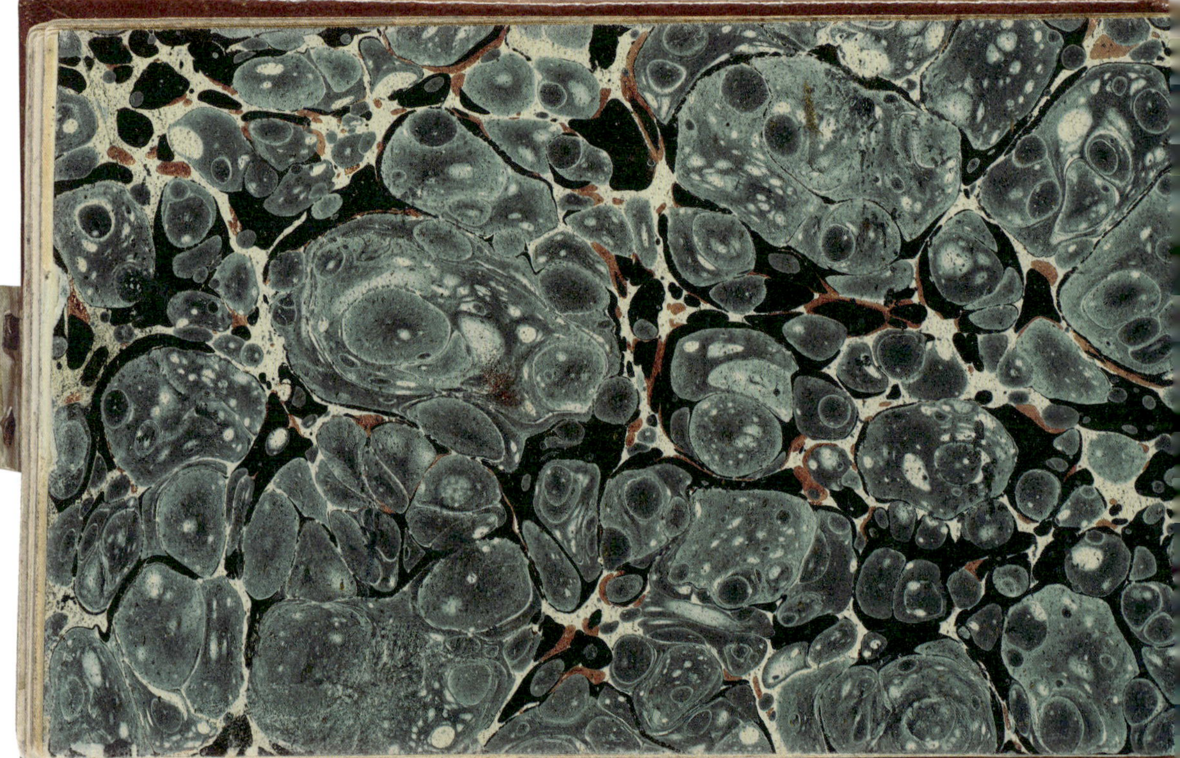

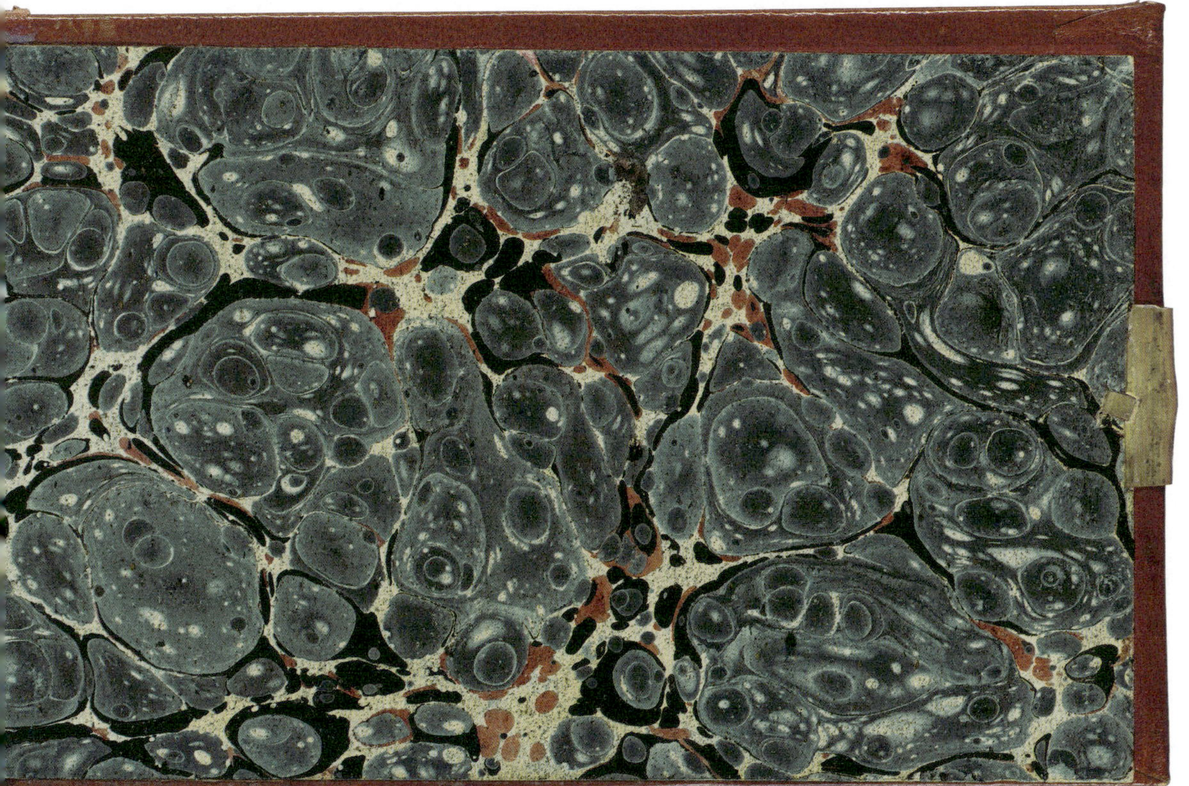

About the Sketchbook

THIS FACSIMILE reproduces the last known intact sketchbook of Joseph Mallord William Turner (1775–1851). Acquired by the Yale Center for British Art (YCBA) in 1986, it is one of more than three hundred used by Turner over his lifetime. A small green label on the inside front cover reveals that it was purchased from William Pilsworth, a commercial stationer in London. Pilsworth's shop in Pudding Lane was conveniently located en route to the dock where Turner regularly caught the steamboat to Margate.

The artist seldom left home without drawing materials, which he used to sketch, make color studies, and jot observations about land, sea, light, and atmosphere. The contents of the sketchbook date from June to September 1845. Turner very likely used it on the coast of the English Channel in Kent, probably exclusively in Margate, just before he departed for northern France. Due to his failing health, Turner's trip to the continent that September would be his last.

"Pocketbooks," with measurements of approximately four by seven inches, were generally intended for recordkeeping rather than sketching and were used in a vertical orientation. As the term suggests, a book of this size could easily be carried in a coat pocket and held open in one hand while writing or drawing with the other. Turner rotated the book to hold it horizontally and made watercolor sketches on the right-hand leaves (up to 67R). He then turned it upside down to work from back to front. The resulting studies from nature include the progress of a single sunset and identifiable topography in and around Margate, such as Droit House on the old pier. Other sketches appear to depict storm-tossed or foundering ships, or whale hunts. These renderings share the abstract, ethereal quality of the artist's paintings of the period.

The sketchbook was presumably among the materials in the possession of Sophia Caroline Booth, Turner's partner for the last part of his life, either at their home in Cheyne Walk, Chelsea, or at the cottage in Margate where Turner first rented a room from Booth in the late 1820s or early 1830s.

Although the early ownership history of the sketchbook is not certain, it is believed that the artist and critic John Ruskin, an admirer of Turner, obtained it directly from Booth. When Ruskin inventoried Turner's works, he described it as Turner's "last sketchbook in colours." In the 1880s, Laurence William Hodson acquired the sketchbook, possibly from Ruskin or an intermediate owner. Hodson's descendants consigned it to Sotheby's in 1986.

When the sketchbook came up for sale, Duncan Robinson, then the director of the YCBA, recognized its significance. He encouraged the museum's founder, Paul Mellon, to purchase it. John Baskett, Mellon's art adviser, bid on his behalf but was outbid. When it was rumored that the sketchbook might be disbound and sold sheet by sheet by a London dealer, Robinson persuaded Mellon to secure it.

Although other Turner sketchbooks from the same period have come to light, they are disbound. This one is unique, as the last intact book to have been in private hands. Owing to its remarkable state of preservation, its colors appear as vivid and bright as the day they were laid down.

Nathan Flis

SELECT BIBLIOGRAPHY

Forrester, Gillian. "The Channel Sketchbook," in *Paul Mellon's Legacy: A Passion for British Art*, edited by John Baskett et al., 286, no. 94. New Haven and London: Yale University Press for Yale Center for British Art, 2007.

Moyle, Franny. *The Extraordinary Life and Momentous Times of J. M. W. Turner*. New York: Penguin Press, 2016.

Warrell, Ian. *Turner's Sketchbooks*. London: Tate, 2014.

Wilton, Andrew. *Turner in His Time*. London: Thames & Hudson, 2006.

Published by Yale Center for British Art
britishart.yale.edu

Distributed by Yale University Press
New Haven and London
yalebooks.com / yalebooks.co.uk

Third printing, November 2025

ISBN 9780300275841 / LCCN 2023918277

Design by Julie Fry
Editing by Katharine Baker
Photography by Michael Ipsen and Robert Hixon
Project management by Nathan Flis
Printed and bound in Italy by Trifolio

Front cover: 72v / Back cover: 64r